I0759630

TRANS-AM
CHALLENGERS
THE CARS THAT RIVALLED MUSTANG
& CAMARO SUPREMACY
1966-1972
STEVE HOLMES
SUNOCO
6

AMERICAN MUSCLE & MOTORSPORT

Chevrolet Corvette (John Starkey)
Cranswick on Camaro 1967-81 (Marc Cranswick)
Cranswick on Classic Chevrolet Corvette 1953-96 (Marc Cranswick)
Cranswick on Ford Maverick and Mercury Comet 1970-77 (Marc Cranswick)
Ford Midsize Muscle – Fairlane, Torino & Ranchero (Marc Cranswick)
Ford Mustang II & Pinto (Marc Cranswick)
Ford versus Ferrari (John Starkey)
MOPAR Muscle - Barracuda, Dart & Valiant 1960-1980 (Marc Cranswick)
NISSAN – The GTP & Group C Racecars 1984-1993 (John Starkey)
Pontiac Firebird – The Auto-Biography (Marc Cranswick)
Racing Camaros (Steve Holmes)
Racing Mustangs (Steve Holmes)
The Legend of American Motors (Marc Cranswick)

www.veloce.co.uk

First published in 2025 by Veloce, an imprint of David and Charles Limited. Tel +44 (0)1305 260068 / e-mail info@veloce.co.uk / web www.veloce.co.uk.

ISBN: 9781836440345

Designed and produced by Veloce. Printed and bound in China by Asia Pacific.

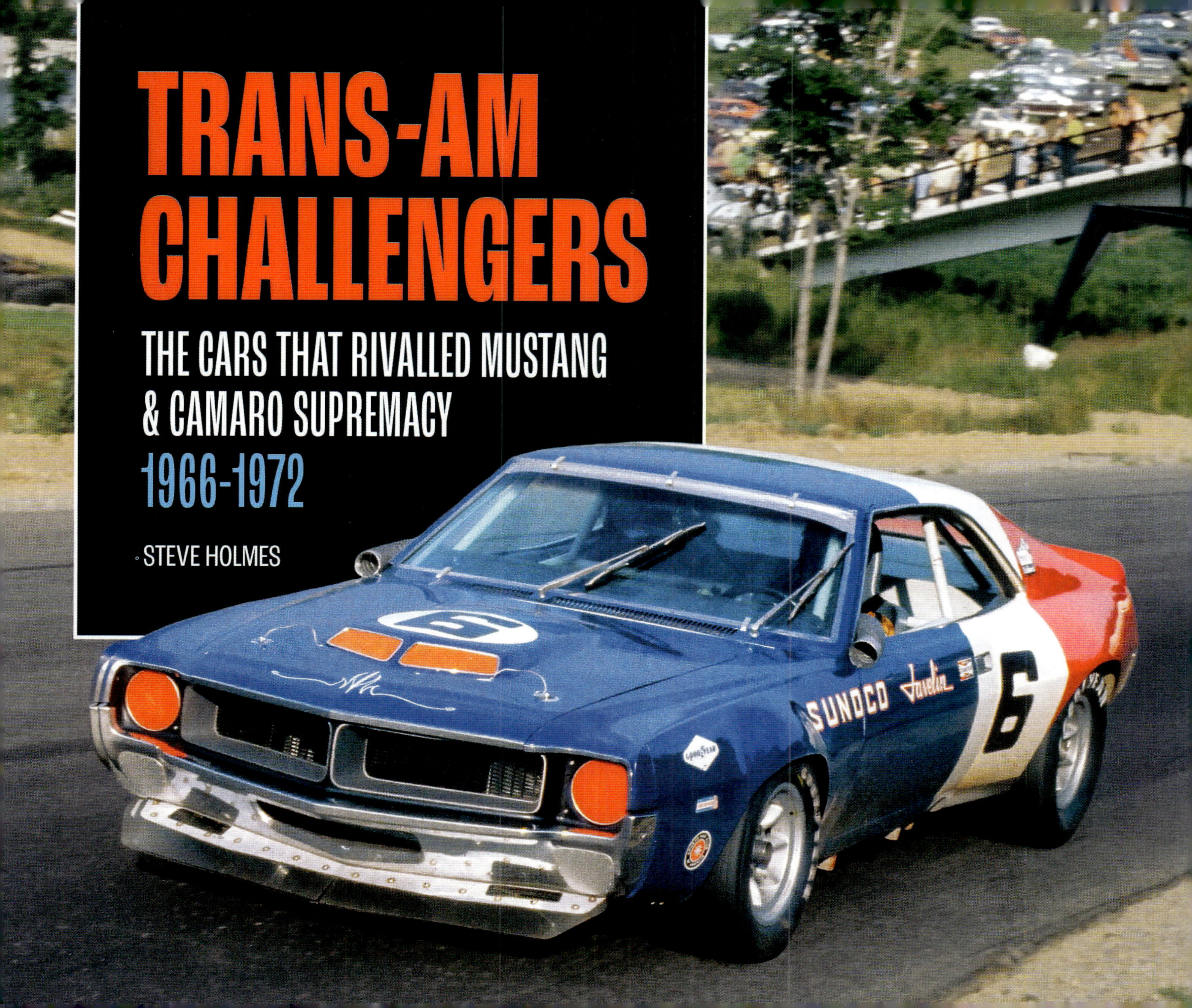
TRANS-AM CHALLENGERS
THE CARS THAT RIVALLED MUSTANG & CAMARO SUPREMACY
1966-1972
STEVE HOLMES
SUNOCO
Javelin
6

Contents

About this book

The Sports Car Club of America (SCCA) Trans-American Sedan Championship is one of the longest-running road racing contests in world motorsport. Since its inception, it has undergone several transformations, and continues to this day.

The Trans-Am has weathered various highs and lows, but has stood the test of time. It also outlasted other, more fancied championships. The SCCA introduced the Trans-Am, the Can-Am Group 7 sports car championship, and the SCCA Grand Prix Championship (Formula A/Formula 5000), all within 12 months. But, a decade later, only the Trans-Am survived.

The greatest era of the Trans-Am was from 1966 to 1972, when the manufacturers were invested and the cars were genuinely relatable to those being driven on the street.

Of course, Ford was first to enter the Trans-Am. It did so in 1966, and won the first Trans-Am Manufacturers' Championship. The story of the Mustang has been told, and that of its closest rival – in showrooms and on the race track – the Chevrolet Camaro.

When the Mustang first came to market in 1964, it generated so much excitement and sold in such numbers that Ford's competition were prompted into action, to design and produce their own versions of the Mustang. And naturally, when the Mustang went racing, the competition had to do likewise. It was the perfect storm.

Because the Trans-Am was based on FIA Group 2 touring car regulations, and then an SCCA-tweaked version of Group 2, manufacturers were required to produce special homologation versions of their base-model pony cars in order to carry across special competition components to help their products on the track.

And while the Mustang and Camaro scored the lion's share of victories and championships during that important 1966-70 period before most of the manufacturers withdrew, the stories of their many, varied rivals are just as compelling.

Across five racing seasons from 1966 to 1970, the SCCA Trans-Am also enjoyed manufacturer support from Dodge, Plymouth, Mercury, American Motors Corporation, and Pontiac. American Motors would outlast them all, and was the only manufacturer still funding a factory Trans-Am program in 1971 and 1972.

This book tells the stories of the manufacturers aside from Ford and Chevrolet (whose stories were told in the Racing Mustangs and Racing Camaros books), and their attempts to topple the big two in the Trans-Am.

This was an exciting, albeit brief era, when pony car sales were at an all-time high, and this very special and truly unique road-racing championship offered the best way to promote the sporting qualities of these vehicles. Sadly, it all ended too soon. The 1970s saw the dawn of a whole new world; one with escalating insurance premiums for performance vehicles, an impending global energy crisis resulting in fuel shortages, and a new generation of youth buyers with quite different requirements.

But while it lasted, the SCCA Trans-Am was a global phenomenon. It boasted some of the best racing drivers on the planet, and the manufacturers invested millions in funding factory race teams and producing some of the most legendary American sports cars of all time.

Acknowledgments

Although I was too young to have witnessed the original 1966 to 1972 SCCA Trans-Am in person, it's a period of US motorsport history I've had a great fascination with since childhood. To that end, I've spent a lifetime collecting anything to do with this great series, and this wonderful era.

I've written three books on the subject – including Racing Mustangs and Racing Camaros – and it's been an incredibly rewarding, enjoyable journey. I thank the team at Veloce Publishing for allowing me the opportunity to share my passion with other enthusiasts.

And, of course, this book could never have been created without the support of those who've generously provided original photographs and period information to help bring this project together. These people include Bill O'Hall, Larry Fulhorst, Harry Hurst, Chad Raynal, Bruce Thompson, Denis Giguère, Doug Morton, Dave Nicholas, Cliff Reuter, Ron Lathrop, Daniel Mensinger, Dominic St-Jean, Michael Keyser at Autosportsltd.com, Doug Dodd, Greg Hansen, Jon Mello, Paul Berkahn, Raynald Bélanger, John Stanley, Dave Nicholas (BARC Boys), Dick Weldon, Stu Brennan, Chris Wiehle, Kevin Skinner, Larry J Honegger, Tom Honegger, and John Gabrial, who provided the superb Trans-Am program covers.

And finally, thank you to my amazing wife Helen, who leads a quite solitary existence, particularly as I race toward my deadlines, but is always hugely supportive and enthusiastic.

Introduction

During its annual meeting at the Statler-Hilton Hotel in Detroit, on 27 January 1966, the Sports Car Club of America (SCCA) announced its plans to launch a new professional road racing championship for sedans. It was called the Trans-American Sedan Championship (Trans-Am), so named because it would span the width of the US with races on the East and West Coasts, and everywhere in between.

This announcement was significant for a number of reasons. Firstly, the SCCA had established itself as a strictly amateur club, and remained so until 1961. But with increased opposition coming from competing governing bodies, the SCCA needed to evolve to survive.

Secondly, by adopting sedan racing, the SCCA ran the very real risk of being associated with stock car racing; the antithesis of everything the Sports Car Club of America stood for. The SCCA, as its name suggests, has its roots in sports car racing.

In 1933, brothers Sam and Miles Collier established the Automobile Racing Club of America (ARCA – not to be confused with the similarly named stock car organization formed in 1953), which was built on the growing popularity of imported British sporty trinkets, with which their amateur owners were keen to indulge in a little spirited road racing competition on weekends. ARCA ended in 1941 as the US entered the war but, three years later, the SCCA rose from its remnants, along with several of its members.

With hostilities ending, the way was clear for the SCCA to focus on hosting its first sanctioned event: the Watkins Glen Grand Prix, in 1948. The sinewy 6.6-mile street course weaved its way around the Watkins Glen State Park and Watkins Glen village, and, naturally, every one of the 35 cars entered had been produced before the war. All but five originated from Europe. The race was won by Frank Griswold Jnr in an Alfa Romeo 8C 2900B. Among the competition was Briggs Cunningham aboard the BuMerc, a 1939 Buick Century disguised beneath a Mercedes-Benz body.

The Watkins Glen street race proved enormously popular among competitors, the public, and the media, despite its perils. Sam Collier was killed during a support race at the 1950 event, as were three spectators. Regardless, the SCCA opted to build upon its achievements, by launching the National Sports Car Championship in 1951. The eight-race series was headlined by the Watkins Glen Grand Prix, and new events at Pebble Beach and Elkhart Lake. The former took place along public roads around Pebble Beach, in Monterey County, California, and was supported by a newly established Concours d'Elegance held on the putting tee and driving range next to the privately owned Beach Club near Del Monte Lodge. Thirty cars took part in what would evolve into one of the world's most extravagant motoring events.

John Fitch won the inaugural SCCA National Sports Car Championship, at the helm of a Briggs Cunningham-entered Jaguar. Much excitement surrounded his achievement, and bragging rights were there for the taking, but Fitch didn't receive any prize money.

The 1950 National Sports Car Championship set the tone for the decade that lay ahead. Indeed, sports car racing grew in stature, and the SCCA held its position at the top of the heap. Naturally, the popularity of its events generated interest from drivers and teams around the globe. And while, initially at least, there were no American sports car manufacturers offering anything that could take the fight to the imports, these contests ultimately spawned an increasing number of locally brewed Specials – one-offs or very low-volume concoctions that grew ever more impressive with each new year. They were wondrous creations like Briggs Cunningham's C-1 through C-6R, the Stroppe Kurtis, Caballo De Hierro, Morgensen Special, Excaliburs, Ken Miles' MG R-1 and R-2 'The Flying Shingle', Troutman-Barnes Special, Barneson-Hagemann-Naruo Chrysler, The Eliminator, Huffaker-Chevy, Max Balchowsky's series of Ol' Yaller's, Bill Sadler's self-named creations, and the lavish Scarabs of Lance Reventlow, son of Woolworths heir Barbara Hutton. Even Chevrolet got in on the act with its exotic Corvette Specials such as the SR-2 and SS.

At the 1964 Sebring 12-Hours endurance event was a preliminary contest called the Sebring 250-Kilometre International Sedan Race, which featured a Le Mans start. Among the wide variety of mostly stock sedans was Augie Pabst in a Holman-Moody Ford Galaxie NASCAR Grand National stock car. The low, broad silhouette of the Galaxie can be seen here alongside the Falcon Sprint of Walt Hansgen. (Courtesy Doug Morton Collection)

No doubt, the 1950s was a very special decade for American sports car racing, and American Specials. And while the SCCA ultimately softened its stance on professional drivers, it stuck resolutely to its amateur racing policy. Of course, that didn't mean teams would necessarily run at a loss. There were always sponsorship opportunities, and car dealerships and garages used SCCA road racing to market their products and services.

But by the end of the decade, the SCCA was batting off increased competition from rival governing bodies. The United States Auto Club (USAC), whose portfolio included the Indianapolis 500, was one of those

Heading into turn 1 for the first time in the 1964 Sebring 250-Kilometre International Sedan Race, the Augie Pabst Galaxie cuts a wide shape. Pabst got away slowly because he had to climb through the window, this being a NASCAR stock car. However, he was leading within two laps, and went on to easily win the race. It was perhaps because of this very car that the SCCA introduced a maximum engine size of 5000cc and maximum wheelbase of 116in when it launched the Trans-Am series two years later, to keep such vehicles away from its events. (Courtesy Doug Morton Collection)

muscling in on the SCCA's sports car racing turf, and USAC was all too happy to offer prize money to attract quality grids. This brought pressure from within the SCCA's own ranks to either evolve or risk bringing about its demise.

SCCA executive director John Bishop headed a small but determined group inside the club pushing for change. But he had a fight on his hands. Several of the old guard wanted to remain a strictly amateur organization. Ultimately, however, common sense prevailed.

Although continuing to host amateur racing events, Bishop and his team

Left: At Waterford Hills in 1964, a typical SCCA sedan race, featuring a variety of makes and models, including Chevrolet Corvair, BMC Mini, Volvo PV544, and VW Beetle. (Courtesy Ron Lathrop)

Below left: Surely one of the first Mustangs to be road raced, pictured here at Waterford Hills in May 1964, and barely fending off a Volvo, with a purposeful Lotus Cortina looming. (Courtesy Ron Lathrop)

focused their efforts on organizing a small number of professional races, teaming up with the local affiliate of the FIA, the Automobile Competition Committee of the United States (ACCUS). From this, a loosely formalized professional competition dubbed the Fall Series was created, hosted by various different track promoters.

The popularity explosion of modified sports car racing prompted the creation of a couple of very important cars in the early 1960s. In 1961, Bob McKee was commissioned by Indy 500 winner Roger Ward to modify a mid-engined Cooper Monaco to accommodate a lightweight aluminum Buick V8 motor.

The Ward Cooper-Buick was revolutionary, and was soon followed by an even more forward-thinking design entered in an SCCA event in October 1962 by a young Roger Penske. With sponsorship from DuPont, the slinky red projectile was named the Zerex Special. Having closely studied the loosely written modified sports car regulations, Penske acquired a Formula 1 Cooper that had suffered damage in the 1961 United States Grand Prix. He had the tube-frame chassis modified for greater rigidity, replaced the 1.5-liter Coventry Climax motor with a 2.7-liter variant, moved the driver's seat a fraction to the left side of the chassis, and fitted a tiny passenger seat off to the right. He then cloaked his creation in a swoopy aluminum body.

Strictly speaking, Penske's little Zerex Special wasn't illegal, but that didn't mean his rivals, or the SCCA, were happy with his willingness to push the boundaries. The SCCA was hit with a slew of complaints, and even visiting internationals threatened to boycott future events. SCCA-modified sports car racing had reached a crucial point, and the regulations weren't keeping up with the pace of development.

To that end, SCCA governing board member Tracy Bird teamed up with Texan oil magnate and fellow racer Jim Hall to nail down a detailed set of regulations going forward. Bird and Hall were both keen sports car racers and advocates of American Specials; Bird had a Cooper Monaco powered by a Ferrari V12, and Hall the Troutman & Barnes-based Chaparral 1.

The updated rules included seating clarification and where those seats were positioned within the vehicle, plus cockpit dimensions, minimum door sizes, and various other points of definition, including that of bodywork. They then submitted the rules to the FIA, which classified them initially under the guise of Group 9, before settling upon Group 7.

Although the Group 7 regulations tied up the many loose ends of the outgoing rule book, there remained enormous scope for car designers to truly go wild. Indeed, Group 7 would offer more creative freedom than just about any other formula of the era. It was with the Group 7 rules that the SCCA launched a new national sports car competition in 1963, called the United States Road Racing Championship (USRRC).

The 1963 USRRC took in eight events and provided hugely exciting racing with packed grids, prompted by the rich prize pool, and its success encouraged Bishop and his team to get even more ambitious.

The January 1966 announcement of the new Trans-Am series preceded another big SCCA announcement the following month: an international Group 7 sports car championship with races in the US and Canada. It was named the Canadian-American Challenge Cup (or Can-Am). In early 1967, the club completed the professional road racing trifecta with its new SCCA Grand Prix Championship for Formula 1, Formula 2, and Formula 3 cars, under the guise of Formula A, Formula B, and Formula C. Unlike the Trans-Am and Can-Am, however, the new open-wheeler series didn't gain much traction during its first season, with the Formula A grid being particularly light on contestants. And so the SCCA tweaked its Formula A regulations to allow the use of 5-liter stock block V8 engines. And with that, Formula A – or Formula 5000 as it became known when adopted elsewhere in the world – truly took off. Because the engines that powered F5000 cars were much the same as those powering the new Trans-Am sedans, engine builders such as Traco Engineering and Al Bartz were already well versed.

John Bishop was a proponent of using FIA regulations wherever possible, and at most SCCA events, including Regionals, cars built to FIA rules were prevalent. Doing so minimized politics within the sport, allowing the SCCA to effectively play the role of promoter. It would also allow international teams to compete in SCCA championship races with cars built to the same set of regulations.

As such, the January 1966 SCCA announcement in Detroit would be that of a Manufacturers' Championship for FIA Appendix J Group 2 Touring Cars. These were to be mass-produced vehicles, with at least 1000 units manufactured within a 12-month period.

Group 2 was a set of regulations established and policed by the FIA. They were in widespread use throughout the racing world, including the European Touring Car Championship, various European national championships, and the Australian Touring Car Championship. The successful British Saloon Car Championship used a set of FIA regulations called Group 5, which were similar to Group 2, but offered a few more freedoms, such as cylinder head and suspension design.

Embracing Group 2 rules simplified matters for the SCCA, because each make and model had to be approved by the FIA before it could compete. This process included a highly detailed set of papers called a homologation sheet, in which everything from the vehicle's dimensions (length, width, height, wheelbase, track), weight, suspension layout, brakes, engine, transmission, and rear end were all listed in the paperwork and photographed, and even included the materials each item was made from. The paperwork for the motor included bore and stroke, total cubic capacity, compression ratio, cylinder head design, materials used, right down to the weight of the bearings and the number of blades on the cooling fan.

The homologation sheet also included any performance components offered by the manufacturer that could be carried across to the race car. These parts had to be supplied with the street car, or sold separately in sufficient numbers by the manufacturer.

Group 2 rules allowed some freedoms that were not shown on the homologation sheet, such as replacement carburetor(s), suspension springs, tires, plus much of the engine internals, although roller rockers were not allowed unless fitted to the street car, and nor could there be a dry-sump system. Bumpers could be removed, and lightweight racing wheels could be installed, as could a racing bucket seat for the driver, and a roll bar.

The SCCA could simply have technical officers check each car upon its arrival at the track, and compare it with its homologation sheet before signing it off to race.

The adoption of Group 2 sedan racing by the SCCA wasn't limited to the new Trans-Am series. Indeed, the SCCA was divided into six different regions, spread throughout the US, and each region already featured sedan competition, albeit, loosely formatted and usually mixed with other classes. For 1966, the sedan division would become official, and split into four classes based on engine size:

D/Sedan: 0-1000cc
C/Sedan: 1001-1300cc
B/Sedan: 1301-2000cc
A/Sedan: 2001-5000cc

The arrival of SCCA sedan racing, and the Trans-Am, coincided neatly with the arrival of Ford's new Mustang which, from its April 1964 launch, set new sales records. However, according to John Bishop, the decision to introduce sedan racing was not as a result of the Ford Mustang's sales success. The goal was always to have a European Touring Car Championship-style competition in the US.

But the SCCA could also see the excitement the Mustang generated would prompt Ford's rivals to quickly bring to market their own Mustang variants, and that could only be a good thing for the Trans-Am. Strictly speaking, the Mustang was a sedan. It had four seats. But it was a very sporty sedan, and one which targeted the youth market; the new generation of baby boomers.

Also, Ford president Lee Iacocca had been proactive in inducting the new Mustang into its massive Total Performance motorsport program, and commissioned Ford-contracted Carroll Shelby to produce a special two-seat version of the fastback, specifically for SCCA B/Production sports car racing, where it'd go head-to-head with Chevrolet's small-block Corvette. As such, it wasn't a stretch to imagine the Mustang in its base notchback body guise also finding a home in this newfangled sedan road racing concept.

Where the SCCA drew the line, however, was in leaving the door open to a potential influx of NASCAR and USAC stock cars. What it needed to avoid at all costs was having 7-liter Galaxies hurtling around close to Mini Coopers and Honda 600s; the damage it would do to the SCCA's reputation could be fatal. To that end, it set the maximum engine size for A/Sedans at 5000cc and a maximum wheelbase of 116in specifically for this reason. Also, and this was important, stock engines larger than 5000cc couldn't be de-stroked or sleeved to bring them within this limit.

Interestingly, in 1963, the British Saloon Car Championship was invaded by a trio of lightweight Ford Galaxies built by Holman-Moody. These cars differed to those competing on the stock car circuit, in that they were built to FIA Group 2 regulations. And they proved virtually unbeatable. But they were run by traditional British teams, such as the John Willment Group and Alan Brown Racing, regular Formula 1 and sports car racing campaigners, and piloted by single-seat and sports car drivers such as Jim Clark, Graham Hill, Jack Brabham, Denny Hulme, and Jack Sears. Although their arrival was relatively unpopular with competing teams and the British Racing & Sports Car Club (which ran the BRSCC), this was largely because they trumped the highly successful British-made Jaguars from the moment they landed. The BRSCC made its feelings known regarding American cars two years earlier when Dan Gurney blitzed the Jags at the International Trophy at Silverstone with a 409in^3 Chevy Impala. He would have won were it not for a broken wheel two laps from the finish. The Impala was thus promptly barred from future competition.

And so it was that the SCCA was going sedan racing. There was a great opportunity to be had, with Ford's rivals in Detroit expected to come to market with their own pony cars within the next couple of years. To that end, the new Trans-Am Championship would be aimed squarely at enticing the manufacturers, and while there would be a Manufacturers' Championship, there wouldn't be a Drivers' Championship. In that respect, it differed to the Can-Am sports car series.

The Trans-Am Championship would be based on SCCA A/B/C/D/Sedan Group 2 regulations, but simplified and split into just two classes:

Under 2000cc
Over 2000cc

The SCCA expected most of its grids would be bolstered by local cars contesting local events as the circus traveled around the US (and Canada from 1968), and competing for a portion of the modest $5000 purse on offer at each race. Here the Trans-Am differed once more to the Can-Am. Factory Lola driver John Surtees reportedly collected $78,000 prize money on his way to winning the inaugural Can-Am Championship. Bruce McLaren wrote in his Autosport column 'From The Cockpit' that he (McLaren Cars) generated more prize money from the six-round Can-Am series in 1966 than from the last three Formula 1 seasons combined! And he didn't even win a race!

The Can-Am was the richest road racing series on the planet. The same couldn't be said for the Trans-Am. The winner in each class would take home $788, with an additional $500 paid to the overall winner. Prize money was awarded down to tenth position in each class ($68), and points were the same as that of Can-Am (and Formula 1): 9-6-4-3-2-1. Points would be awarded within each class, irrespective of where cars finished on track in relation to those in a different class.

Each manufacturer could only score points once in each race. If, for example, Mustangs filled the first three positions in the O2 class and a Plymouth Barracuda was fourth, Ford would be awarded nine points for its lead car, while Plymouth would receive three points.

The 1966 SCCA Trans-Am Championship featured seven rounds, beginning with a 4-Hour endurance race set as a curtain-raiser on the Friday of the annual Sebring 12-Hours on March 25. There followed races at Mid-America Raceway, Bryar Motorsport Park, Virginia International Raceway, Marlboro Park Speedway, Green Valley Raceway, and concluded at Riverside International Raceway on 18 September. These were organized as endurance events. Mid-America Raceway was 300 miles, Bryar was 250 miles. Virginia International Raceway was 400 miles. The Marlboro race was 12 hours, Green Valley six hours, and Riverside four hours.

Prior to announcing the Trans-Am, the SCCA reached out to several manufacturers to garner interest. On 27 January 1966, at the Statler-Hilton Hotel in Detroit, it proudly boasted a list of cars expected to take part, which included the Ford Mustang, Lotus Cortina, Plymouth Barracuda, and Alfa Romeo GTA. Based on SCCA regional events, models such as the Mini Cooper S, BMW 1800, Volvo 122, and Saab 96 should also take part. Certainly, the Trans-Am wasn't about to overshadow the Can-Am, but the SCCA was banking on the series soon growing. How prophetic this was!

1966

Setting the tone for the years that followed, the 1966 SCCA Trans-Am curtain-opener at Sebring boasted some factory support, albeit modest. Much like the European Touring Car Championship (ETCC), British Saloon Car Championship (BSCC), and other international touring car contests, small-bore cars made up the bulk of the grid and enjoyed most of the manufacturer backing.

Bruce McLaren once said, "A good big 'un will always beat a good little 'un." And he was mostly right. But as had been proven in European touring car racing, small-bore cars often had the measure of their big-bore counterparts. Alan Mann Racing contested the entire nine-race 1965 ETCC, usually running two or three cars, and spearheaded by a Lotus Cortina for John Whitmore. But AMR also campaigned a Mustang in five races. Aside from a blown motor in the opening round at Monza, Whitmore won his class in every race that followed, and in doing so, became the 1965 European Touring Car Champion.

The ETCC was split into three classes based on engine size, and while the Lotus Cortina fitted into Division 2, the Mustang ran Division 3. At most events, each Division had its own separate race. But an interesting comparison between the AMR Mustang and Lotus Cortina could be made at the Nürburgring in Germany, Karlskoga in Sweden, and Zandvoort in the Netherlands, where Divisions 2 and 3 were combined into a single grid, albeit with drivers only scoring class points. In two of the three combined races, the AMR Mustang, driven by the Swede Bo Ljungfeldt, finished ahead. Also, Divisions 2 and 3 ran together at Mont Ventoux in France, and although AMR didn't enter its own Mustang, there were other Mustang teams in the race. All of them were defeated by the flying Whitmore Lotus Cortina.

While Alan Mann Racing was busy flying the Ford of Britain flag in the ETCC, the BSCC provided another interesting comparison between the Lotus Cortinas, which were the fastest small-bore cars, and the Mustangs. The eight-round 1965 BSCC was split into four classes, based on engine size:

The first SCCA Trans-Am race was contested as a 4-Hour curtain-raiser for the 1966 Sebring 12-Hours, and made very little impact. However, it did somehow end up on the cover of *Autosport* magazine.

Class A: 0-1000cc
Class B: 1001-1300cc
Class C: 1301-2000cc
Class D: Over 2000cc

Aside from its 5000cc maximum engine cap for the big-bore class, the SCCA adopted this exact same formula when it introduced Group 2 Sedan racing in 1966. And as the SCCA would do with its new Trans-Am Championship in 1966, BSCC races would combine all classes into a single

Alan Mann Racing, from England, committed to a full schedule in the inaugural SCCA Trans-Am, starting here at Sebring, where two cars were entered. #44, seen here, was driven by John Whitmore, who was fresh from having won the 1965 European Touring Car Championship aboard an Alan Mann Racing Lotus Cortina. (Courtesy Doug Morton Collection)

The second AMR Lotus Cortina was driven by Peter Procter. Both cars failed to finish at Sebring. (Courtesy Doug Morton Collection)

grid, with points paid on class finishing positions, rather than overall positions.

Alan Mann Racing played an indirect role in the 1965 BSCC. In 1964, it had campaigned a team of Mustangs in the Tour de France endurance road rally, and at the end of the year, converted these cars to FIA Group 2 specification for road racing duties. Roy Pierpoint and Mike Salmon would race two of them in the 1965 BSCC, while former Ford Galaxie racer Gawaine Baillie would drive a third.

Meanwhile, Team Lotus and the John Willment Group would run factory Lotus Cortinas. Team Lotus entered examples for Jim Clark and Jack Sears, although Clark only ran a limited campaign, with his Formula 1 commitments taking priority. Frank Gardner drove the Willment car.

Mustangs finished first in six of the eight races, with Clark showing his star quality by taking victory in the wet Goodwood race, coming home first from team-mate Sears. Clark also took pole position in the opening encounter at Brands Hatch, but was struck out by an engine failure in the race. Jack Brabham won the penultimate round at Brands Hatch in the Alan Brown-entered Mustang, and also crossed the line first in the final at Oulton Park, only to be disqualified after the race for running oversized valves. Clark was the beneficiary of Brabham's disqualification.

Although the Mustangs and Lotus Cortinas contested different classes, the comparable performances between them suggested the SCCA might actually have an exciting proposition on its hands. This was heightened when Alan Mann Racing confirmed it would run a brace of Lotus Cortinas in the inaugural Trans-Am Championship.

Autodelta SpA, the Alfa Romeo competition department, sent two Alfa

GTAs to Sebring for 1965 Le Mans 24 Hours winner (and future Formula 1 World Champion) Jochen Rindt to share with Roberto Bussinello, while a second entry was driven by Andrea de Adamich/Teodoro Zeccoli. There were another four independent GTAs.

Three Mustangs were entered in the Sebring race, headed by Dale Wood's example driven by A J Foyt, plus those of Ed Diamond and Dick Thompson. But none were factory cars. Ford had no plans to bankroll a factory Trans-Am effort in 1966. However, Shelby American would support Ford's goal to win the Trans-Am Manufacturers' Championship by building turn-key Group 2 Mustang notchbacks for anyone prepared to stump up the $5500 asking price, much like it had done previously with the Shelby GT350 in SCCA B/ Production sports car racing the year prior. But likewise, none of the three Mustangs at Sebring were Shelby-built cars.

A total of 43 cars took the start of the Sebring Trans-Am race, of which only nine contested the O2 class. Aside from the three Mustangs, there were three Plymouth Barracudas, two Chevrolet Corvairs, and one Dodge Dart. The lone Dart was the Group 44 entry driven by Bob Tullius (owner of Group 44) and Tony Adamowicz, and was the most competitive O2 car behind the Foyt Mustang. The three Barracudas were those of Scott Harvey, Charlie Rainville/Bruce Jennings (both Team Starfish entries),

Roger West raced just about anything with four wheels, including speedway cars. He drove this BMC Mini Cooper in the first Trans-Am at Sebring, finishing 13th outright and tenth in the U2 class. The nose of A J Foyt's Mustang, which would lead most of the Sebring race, can be seen here behind the Mini during tech inspection. (Courtesy Doug Morton Collection)

Team Starfish was the factory Plymouth team in the 1966 Trans-Am, campaigning a pair of Barracudas. Scott Harvey was the motivational force behind Team Starfish, and he also drove this Barracuda at Sebring. All the Mopars in 1966 rolled on steel wheels in the early races. Bumpers were removed, as the rules allowed, while mesh covered the radiator. These were basic cars compared with what was to come. A simple roll hoop and side-exit exhausts were among the limited modifications. (Courtesy BARC Boys)

Not wanting to be outdone by Plymouth, Dodge also supported a factory team in the 1966 Trans-Am. Bob Tullius, of Group 44, was chosen to represent the brand. However, the deal came together late, and the Group 44 Dart was completed barely in time for Sebring. Regardless, Tullius finished second outright at Sebring, and first in the O2 class. (Courtesy BARC Boys)

Moments after the start of the 1966 Sebring 4-Hour race, which was the first Trans-Am contest. The cars were gridded in order of engine size, rather than qualifying times. One of the Team Starfish Barracudas leapt to the front, although this would be short-lived. A J Foyt in the Mustang, running second here, soon took the lead and drove away, until a head gasket failed. (Courtesy William A Jordan Collection)

The second of the Team Starfish Barracudas was driven at Sebring by Charlie Rainville and Bruce Jennings. The pair finished seventh outright, and third in O2. (Courtesy Doug Morton Collection)

and Bill Stoutenberg. Spurgeon May and Don Eichsteadt piloted the pair of Corvairs.

The cars were gridded in order of engine size, rather than practice times, and from the start Foyt shot away to build a commanding lead, but retired with head gasket failure on lap 32, and when the checkered flag waved at the end of 67 laps, it wasn't any of the O2 cars in front. Instead, it was Rindt's Alfa GTA, which he drove solo after team-mate Bussinello blotted his copybook and rolled it in practice, requiring it be crudely beaten back into the approximate shape of an Alfa GTA. The top-placed O2 entry was the Group 44 Dodge Dart of Tullius and Adamowicz, which was second on the road, but which won its class. Tullius was driving the last stint and was catching the Alfa, but decided a class win was better than pushing his equipment and not finishing the race.

Plymouth Barracuda

In the 1966 Trans-Am O2 class, the only factory-supported squads to contest the full championship were Team Starfish for Plymouth, and Group 44 for Dodge, but to label this a genuine factory program is being mightily generous. Chrysler really had no interest in going sports car racing, and as such, its support was mostly limited to parts supply and donor cars, plus a little cash.

Plymouth gained traction before Dodge. It launched the quirky Barracuda on 1 April 1964, two weeks before Ford's new Mustang hit the market. Plymouth was targeting the same youth customers as Mustang, but the overwhelming enthusiasm for the Ford pony car largely overshadowed Chrysler's efforts.

The Barracuda was based on the second-generation Plymouth Valiant platform, and its 106in wheelbase was 2in shorter than the 108 of the Mustang, which would quickly become the pony car standard. With the purse strings held tight, transforming the hugely conservative Valiant into something stylish, sporty, and engaging was always going to be a tall order. What they concocted was typically polarizing early-1960s Chrysler fare.

Although the Barracuda was hobbled with the Valiant's front, A-pillars, doors from the pillarless two-door models, bumpers, and rear quarters, the pillarless doors offered some freedom from the B-pillars back, with the Plymouth stylists arriving at a massive rear wraparound window that basically filled the entire rear space.

The Barracuda was offered with a pair of Slant-Six motors and a 273in^3 V8, which fit comfortably within the Trans-Am maximum but was a full 16in^3 smaller than that of the Mustang. The Barracuda was marginally lighter at

Two Chevy Corvairs started the Sebring race, including this example for Don Eichsteadt, which failed to finish. The air-cooled Corvair, at 2486cc, was barely half the size of the Ford and Mopar V8s it was forced to compete against in the O2 class, and as such, was little more than an interesting grid-filler. (Courtesy William A Jordan Collection)

2595lb (1177kg) compared with the 2606 (1182kg) of the Mustang, but the Mustang's larger motor and potentially greater power would more than offset this.

Scott Harvey was part of Chrysler's Product Planning department, and had arranged for mechanics there to build him a Barracuda rally car. The excitable Harvey, known as 'Hot Scarvey' among his peers, was responsible for getting the Barracuda homologated for racing, and when the SCCA announced the Trans-Am series for 1966, so Harvey convinced Chrysler to provide him with a small budget and three Barracuda street cars.

Fittingly, Harvey named his Trans-Am program Team Starfish, and arranged a corner of Chrysler engine development engineer Steve Baker's workshop to build and prepare the cars. Baker would oversee engine building, while Bob Tarozzi, a Chrysler Institute student with racing experience, constructed the cars.

As was accepted under the Group 2 rules, the Barracudas were bereft of bumpers, and fitted with a single roll hoop mounted behind the driver, who snuggled into a lightweight bucket seat. The Chryslers produced approximately 330hp in race trim, around 30 less than the Mustangs. Spent gases exited through pipes dumping out either side ahead of the rear wheels.

Left: The #14 factory Barracuda leads the factory Alfa GTA, entered by Autodelta SpA, and driven by the brilliant Jochen Rindt. Rindt drove solo in the Sebring race after team-mate Roberto Bussinello rolled the car in practice, prompting a hasty repair job using hammers and brute force. (Courtesy William A Jordan Collection)

Below: A third Barracuda raced at Sebring – the independent entry of Bill Stoutenberg. It failed to finish, unlike Scott Harvey, giving chase, who placed sixth outright and second in O2. (Courtesy William A Jordan Collection)

The first SCCA Trans-Am race was won not by a V8 sedan from Detroit, but an Alfa Romeo GTA. Here, Jochen Rindt celebrates his victory. Until 1970 when the U2 and O2 cars were separated into their own races, this was to be one of only two outright wins for a U2 car. (Courtesy William A Jordan Collection)

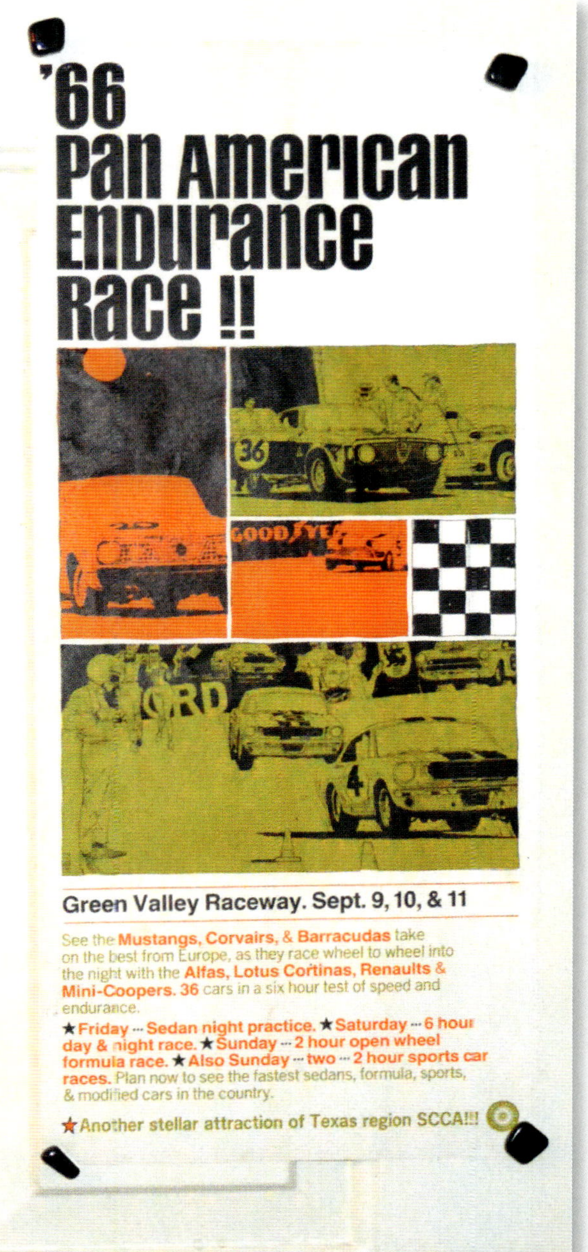

Above: Early in the Green Valley Trans-Am. This curious little track was built around a drag strip, from which a road course was cobbled together using sections of the return and service roads. It was on this track in Texas that Carroll Shelby opted to debut the very first Shelby GT350, in February 1965, with Ken Miles at the wheel. On a rainy day in September 1966, a six-hour Trans-Am contest took place, in front of very few spectators, and with hazards seemingly everywhere. The Charlie Rainville/Bob Johnson Team Starfish Barracuda seen here leads the John McComb/Brad Brooker, which won the race. (Courtesy Jerry Melton)

Top right: The lone Corvair in the Green Valley race was that shared by Spurgeon May and Bill Clay. It failed to go the distance. (Courtesy Jerry Melton)

Middle right: Bob Tullius and Tony Adamowicz shared the Group 44 Dodge to finish sixth outright and fourth in O2. (Courtesy Jerry Melton)

Right: The Rainville/Johnson Barracuda slithered its way to third outright and second in O2 at Green Valley, behind the McComb Mustang, and Gaston Andrey/Horst Kwech Alfa GTA. (Courtesy Jerry Melton)

In early races, the Barracudas had wide steel wheels, before switching to Kelsey-Hayes and magnesium American Racing Wheels, and the car's ride height dropped noticeably closer to the track as the season progressed.

Team Starfish entered two Barracudas in each of the seven-race Trans-Am series, with Charlie Rainville, Bruce Jennings, and Harvey doing the bulk of the driving. The team didn't win any Trans-Am races outright, but Jennings finished second on the road in Round three at Bryar, behind Allan Moffat's factory Lotus Cortina, which earned Plymouth top points for the O2 class.

A handful of other teams campaigned Barracudas in selected 1966 races, including those driven by Bill Stoutenberg, Bill Owens/Bob Spooner, Steve Durst/Al Schall, Peter Hutchinson/Alan Barker, and Dale Maher/Norm Smith. But the Team Starfish entrants were the only ones that ever looked like challenging for race wins.

Dodge Dart

Although mechanically identical to the Barracuda, the third-generation Dodge Dart sported a longer 111in wheelbase, as per Chrysler nameplate hierarchy.

With Scott Harvey having already got the Team Starfish Trans-Am program up and running, Dodge Division decided it didn't want to get left out. Dodge vice-president Bob McCurry instructed B F 'Moon' Mullins and Frank Wylie at Dodge Public Relations to cobble together a Trans-Am program, and Mullins asked Harvey if he could recommend someone to assemble and run it. Harvey suggested Bob Tullius at Group 44.

Tullius already had some backing from Quaker State, and Dodge supplied a new Dart, plus $500 per race. Unlike Team Starfish, Group 44 would function as a one-car team, with Tullius as the driver, and Tony 'A to Z' Adamowicz joining him in every race except Bryar, where Tullius drove solo. The Dodge Trans-Am program came together so late the team barely made it in time for the opening race at Sebring.

Tullius only had three crew members at the start of 1966, so Team Starfish helped with pit stops in the early races. But as Group 44 began to establish itself as the leading Chrysler team, a small rivalry developed. Following their second outright at Sebring (and first in O2), Tullius and Adamowicz scored their breakthrough victory in Round five at Marlboro, and finished second outright in the final at Riverside. Given their late start, it was a pretty decent performance.

From Round two of the championship, a second Dart arrived for *Car and Driver* editor Brock Yates, built by celebrated Mopar NASCAR Grand National constructor Ray Nichols. The Yates-Dart program was organized by Moon Mullins, and was expected to contest the 1966 Daytona 24 Hours race that preceded Sebring, but build delays finally saw it debut in the second Trans-Am at Mid-America Raceway, with Yates sharing driving duties with Chuck Krueger. Being a stock car builder, Nichols essentially created a miniature Grand National car, which ensured it didn't do anything particularly well in a road racing environment. Changes were made for the next race at Bryar, but mechanical failure retired the Dart on lap 59 of 156. NASCAR driver David Pearson joined Yates at Virginia International Raceway, but a blown motor in practice, and no spare, meant the pairing didn't start the race. Krueger and Hal Keck shared the Dart in the 12-Hour race at Marlboro, and finished fourth in a Chrysler clean sweep of the top four positions.

A third Dodge-supported Dart was that of Ron Grable, but it didn't appear until the penultimate race at Green Valley, where it finished fourth.

Chevrolet Corvair

By the time the SCCA Trans-Am Championship debuted in 1966, Chevrolet's Corvair was into its second generation. The Corvair was originally conceived as an economy offering, built to tackle the VW Beetle, which was making great inroads within the American market, and was comparably mean-spirited in its delivery. But the handsome second-generation model was something of a technical marvel, sporting fully independent rear suspension, and the option of a turbocharger hanging off the side of its air-cooled flat-6 engine. Indeed, when Ford was coming to market with its Mustang in 1964, General Motors (GM) acquired an example for assessment, and deemed it inferior in just about every way to the second-gen Corvair.

But smug GM management massively underestimated the Mustang's popularity with the American public, and when the Trans-Am series swung into life in March 1966, Chevrolet was already well advanced in developing its own variant of the Mustang: the Camaro, which would launch in September.

Also by 1966, GM had inflicted upon itself a strict no-racing policy, turning its back on the sport in all its forms, and had no interest in any involvement with the Trans-Am. But surprisingly, a handful of Corvairs contested selected Trans-Am races in 1966, including those of Spurgeon May and Don Eichsteadt at Sebring, where both cars, naturally, underwhelmed. Eichsteadt broke an input shaft and retired, while May finished 19th of the 26 cars still circulating, including the walking wounded.

May teamed up with Donna Mae-Simms at Marlboro, while Eichsteadt joined forces with Tony DeLorenzo, whose father was vice-president for Public Relations at GM, and who would go on to achieve considerable success campaigning big-block Corvettes in SCCA A/Production sports car racing. At Marlboro, the two Corvairs were classified 23rd and 26th from 27 finishers. May fronted for the next race at Green Valley, but failed to finish. That concluded the Corvair chapter in the Trans-Am.

The Corvair may have featured a good rear suspension design, but its 2683cc flat-6 fell well short of the cubic capacity of even the Chrysler pairing, and offered little scope for performance upgrades. The pretty Chevy coupes were, however, an interesting addition to a hugely varied mix of cars competing in the 1966 Trans-Am.

Ford Falcon Sprint

A pair of Ford Falcon Sprints contested the 1966 SCCA Trans-Am series. Jim Taylor's first-generation model and Pete Cordts' second-gen were already obsolete models even before the SCCA announced its plans for the Trans-Am series in early 1966. Ford launched its third-generation Falcon in late 1965, but it hadn't been homologated for racing, unlike its predecessors.

The Falcon was created as a bare-bones compact in 1959, and was finally spiced up a little with the arrival of the handsome Sprint, four years later. Packing the new compact 260in^3 V8, the Sprint was conceived as part of Ford's Total Performance program, where a fleet of Holman-Moody-built examples were sent to Europe to contest the 1963 Monte Carlo Rally, where they performed strongly.

When the second-generation Falcon arrived in late 1963, so Ford again had Holman-Moody build several examples for European endurance rallying. These were homologated with lightweight fiberglass body panels, including the hood, deck lid, fenders, and doors, and listed at a minimum racing weight of 980kg (2160lb) on the homologation sheet which, of course, was a complete fantasy. Now packing a larger 289 motor, Falcons stormed the 1964 Monte Carlo, winning several special stages.

With the arrival of the new Mustang, so it replaced the Falcon in the 1964 Liege-Sofia-Liege and Tour de France rallies, and the Monte Carlo Falcons, campaigned by Alan Mann Racing in Europe, were disbursed to various British race teams, which upcycled them for FIA Group 5 touring car racing, and proceeded to dominate the BSCC until they were outlawed in 1970.

Jim Taylor raced his Falcon Sprint in the 1966 Green Valley Trans-Am race, finishing 17th. Pete Cordts contested the last Trans-Am of 1966, at Riverside, where he and team-mate Jim Dittmore placed a credible ninth. Unlike the European Falcons, the Cordts example didn't have the fiberglass fenders and doors, but it did have a fiberglass hood and deck lid.

Of course, with the arrival of the Mustang in 1964, the new pony car would become the focus for Ford's road racing programs, and the Falcon would return to its original role as a multifaceted, affordable compact.

1966 Trans-Am

Ford ultimately won the first SCCA Trans-Am Manufacturers' Championship, although it very nearly didn't. Had it actually been serious about winning, Chrysler would have placed all its focus into campaigning either Plymouth Barracudas or Dodge Darts, not both. In the end, the inter-Chrysler rivalry ensured the Plymouth and Dodge teams stole points from one another, and even though Ford didn't fund a factory team in the series, its decision to have Shelby American build and supply turn-key Group 2 race cars to independent teams made the difference.

But even then, the 1966 Trans-Am Over-2 Manufacturers' Championship was close. Entering the final race at Riverside, Plymouth and Ford were tied on 37 points. Ford instructed Shelby to enter one of its Mustangs in the Riverside race. Shelby driver Jerry Titus was at the controls. He took pole position and, despite flooding the motor at the Le Mans start, which relegated him almost to the rear of the field, he was already back up to third position by lap six. He quickly pushed to the front and proceeded to lap the entire field, other than Shelby American mechanic Don Pike, in another Mustang.

Titus looked to have the race under control until he pitted to have a leaking oil filter tightened. This lost him several laps, and he rejoined in seventh position, but quickly surged forward once more, eventually retaking the lead, and won the race from Tullius, and Ron Dykes' Mustang.

Titus' victory ensured Ford won the 1966 Over-2 Trans-Am Championship. Interestingly, had the Plymouth and Dodge teams run as one manufacturer, Chrysler would have taken the title, with 49 points to the eventual 46 of Ford. But Chrysler didn't really care.

In late 1966, Chrysler informed Scott Harvey and Bob Tullius that it wouldn't be supporting a Trans-Am program in 1967. It was already heavily committed to its NASCAR Grand National stock car racing and NHRA Super Stock drag racing programs, and siphoning off money and technical support from either to continue in the Trans-Am, which generated very little public interest by comparison, made little sense. Mopar fans would have to wait until 1970 before a truly dedicated Chrysler Trans-Am program arrived.

1967

It was an encouraging start, if not especially earth-shattering. Compared with the 1966 Sports Car Club of America Can-Am Group 7 sports car series, the inaugural Trans-American Sedan Championship slipped by almost unnoticed. But that was all about to change in 1967.

When John Bishop and his team at the SCCA first mooted the concept of the Trans-Am, they did so thinking the series would replicate touring car in Europe and Great Britain. And in 1966, they were right! But 1967 hinted at a new focus for the Trans-Am, one driven by the gradual increase of manufacturer support coming from Detroit. And the motivation for this was the Ford Mustang.

When the Mustang came to market, it set new sales records. After its launch on 17 April 1964, an estimated 4 million people stormed Ford showrooms in the first week alone, just to get a look at the car and test drive it. Ford sold 100,000 Mustangs in the first four months and, by the end of 1965, that figure swelled to over 680,000. Only 12 months later, 1.3 million Mustangs had found buyers, and in 1966, the best year ever for Mustang sales, Ford dealers rolled more than 607,000 out the door. Mustangs accounted for 28 per cent of Ford sales for its total vehicle fleet.

Automotive manufacturers are not driven by emotion. They're in the business of selling motor vehicles – as many as they can. Record-breaking Mustang sales captured the attention of Ford's rivals, who began designing their own Mustang variants. It wasn't because of the way the Mustang looked, or drove, or the interest it generated from the public. It was purely because the Mustang sold in such numbers that it would be remiss of any manufacturer not to act. And thus, throughout the second half of the 1960s, an entirely new market took shape, based on the Mustang theme. Naturally, it was dubbed the 'pony car' market.

Famously, despite General Motors engineers assessing a new Mustang in early 1964 and dismissing it as an inferior product to the second-generation Corvair, by August, approval was given to design and produce a Chevrolet variant of the Mustang. Impressively, from concept to fruition, it went on sale just two years and one month later, on 29 September 1966. It was called the Camaro.

Four days later, Lincoln-Mercury hit the market with its own upmarket pony car: the Mercury Cougar.

Mercury Cougar

1960s Detroit boasted carefully structured market segmenting within each corporation. The concept was that a young, blue-collar worker would buy themselves a Ford, and as they worked their way up the corporate chain, so the quality of their vehicle would follow suit. Within Ford Motor Company, Mercury was the next step, with Lincoln at the top.

To that end, a Mercury Cougar should offer more frills than a Mustang. And indeed, the 1967 Cougar sported foldaway headlights hidden behind a baleen grille (that some in the Trans-Am pit lane likened to a Norelco shaver), various upmarket trimmings, bells and whistles, plushy interior, and importantly, a longer wheelbase, at 111in. In 1960s America, nothing shouted opulence more than a long wheelbase. Naturally, the Cougar was also more expensive. This was, after all, a Mercury, and not a lowly Ford!

Regardless, a Mercury Cougar was just a fancy Mustang, and the two shared most mechanical components. Also, when the Cougar came to market, so it was absorbed into Ford's Total Performance racing program, with a factory team ready for the 1967 SCCA Trans-Am, where it would compete against the Mustang and Chevrolet's new Camaro.

The Mercury Trans-Am project was overseen by the brilliant former hot rodder Fran Hernandez, and he called upon stock car racing icon Bud Moore to run the program. Straight away, this was a notable shift from the tradition of assigning the task to a sports car team.

Dearborn Steel Tubing was contracted to convert a pair of Mercury Cougar street cars into Trans-Am racers, which would then be handed over

to Bud Moore Engineering to finish as its own and campaign throughout the season. Dearborn Steel Tubing was Ford's early skunkworks operation, which took on specialized operations the mothership was too big and cumbersome to do itself. Among its other roles was the modifying of Ford Fairlanes and Mercury Comets for fitment of 427in^3 big-block powerplants in Ford's 1964 NHRA drag racing program.

Bud Moore Engineering immediately benefited from Shelby American having raced the Mustang for the last two years, and everything Shelby learned was passed on to BME. But likewise, Bud Moore and his guys brought a quite different approach to Trans-Am racing. Coming from a stock car racing background, the BME Cougars were built strong and rigid, carrying a distinctive forward rake with the nose buried in the ground to help improve top speed, and to limit air flow beneath the car.

The traditional sports car teams installed a very basic roll bar design aft of the driver almost as an afterthought, the single purpose of which was to provide some protection should the car be flipped on its lid. Bud Moore Engineering, however, recognized that the roll cage could also enhance performance, by connecting all four wheels together. This was common practice in stock car racing. When the BME Cougars rolled out of the transporter for the opening 1967 Trans-Am at Daytona, they sported a much more complex and robust roll cage than even the Shelby Mustangs. It took

Above: The first race of the 1967 Trans-Am was held at Daytona, on the road course layout. And how the landscape had evolved. Chrysler withdrew what little support it offered, but Chevrolet and Mercury stepped in, and suddenly the Trans-Am became one of the most fiercely contested road racing championships on the planet. Here the two factory Bud Moore Engineering Cougars, driven by Parnelli Jones and Dan Durney, lead the pace lap. (Courtesy Revs Institute/Eric della Faille)

Opposite, top: Sebring hosted Round two of the 1967 Trans-Am. This was the Sebring 4-Hour race, which ran prior to the 12-Hour contest. Jerry Titus was on pole in the Shelby American factory Mustang, sporting its yellow paint for the first time, while alongside is Parnelli Jones. After four hours, Titus was still in front. (Courtesy Motoring-man.com)

Opposite: NSU Prinz leads BMC Mini, Fiat Abarth, and Lotus Cortina. The early Trans-Am races were nothing if not diverse. (Courtesy Doug Morton Collection)

their rivals a few races to twig. But, by mid-season, both the Shelby cars and the new Penske Racing Camaros all featured Bud Moore-style roll cages.

Another Bud Moore trick was to droop the noses. A section of metal above the radiator support was removed, which tapered back along the inner fenders toward the firewall, allowing the forward portion of the front fenders to droop, and assisting with top-end speed. Theoretically. Rival teams eventually cottoned on to this stunt as well, and did likewise.

And of course, Bud Moore introduced the sporty car guys to the art of acid-dipping metal components to help shed weight. And not just hoods and fenders, but entire bodyshells! Acid-dipping was, as the term suggests, leaving components submerged in a tank of acid which would eat away at the metal, thus reducing its weight. This was a common trick in stock car racing, but unheard of in sports car racing. The strength of the metal would be somewhat compromised, but this was more than offset by the addition of the roll cage.

Naturally, the Bud Moore Cougars were painted like mini stock cars, with a two-tone hue of maroon and silver, and 'Mercury Cougar' script splashed across the rear flanks. For the first Trans-Am race of 1967, the

Cougars rolled on reinforced steel wheels – another stock car approach where strength is all-important. By Round two they were sporting Kelsey-Hayes wheels, and by Round three had switched to magnesium American Racing Wheels, as per the Shelby team and, for that matter, every other O2 Trans-Am team as well. So, while Bud Moore Engineering was something of a trailblazer with all its stock car tricks, by the same token, it was also learning from the sports car guys.

Most Trans-Am drivers in 1967 hailed from a sports car racing background and followed strict sports car racing etiquette: don't run into the other cars! But Bud Moore hired drivers who had no problem getting their elbows out, roughing up the competition. A plug-and-play system was employed, rotating several different drivers through the two Cougars, many of which hailed from Ford's global racing operation. Not surprisingly, given Bud Moore's roots, Ford's NASCAR Grand National program worked in a similar way.

Among the BME driver line-up in 1967 were NASCAR Grand National hardmen David Pearson, Cale Yarborough, and LeeRoy Yarbrough. Parnelli Jones was a tough all-rounder with USAC and stock car racing experience, and while Dan Gurney raced at the highest level of the sport in Formula 1,

Above: British rallying ace Paddy Hopkirk shared this BMC Mini in the Sebring 4-Hour Trans-Am with John Rhodes. The pair finished 20th outright and sixth in U2. While U2 cars greatly outnumbered O2 cars in the 1966 Trans-Am, the balance became far more even in 1967. (Courtesy Doug Morton Collection)

Opposite, top: Moments after the start of the 1967 Green Valley Trans-Am. The organizers opted for a Le Mans-style start, with drivers running across the track to their cars for some added drama. Both the weather and spectator numbers were a huge improvement on the grim 1966 event. (Courtesy Jerry Melton)

Opposite: Apparently Ron Dykes was the fastest Trans-Am driver in a foot race. He sprinted across the track and into his Mustang before anyone else. Freddy Van Beuren and Dan Gurney give chase. (Courtesy Jerry Melton)

he too was regularly called upon by Ford for rough-and-tumble stock car assignments, most notably on the road courses.

Firestone

QUAKER STATE
44
AS

Far left: Gurney and Jones finished first and second at Green Valley in their BME Cougars. But first they had to beat Ron Dykes' Mustang. (Courtesy Jerry Melton)

Left: When Ford Motor Company decided to go motor racing, it hired the best people in the business to get the job done. That included its drivers. Dan Gurney (left) and Parnelli Jones were international superstars, and Gurney would win a Formula 1 World Championship race this same season in his own Eagle MkI. Having drivers of this caliber gave the Trans-Am instant credibility in 1967. Their busy schedules precluded them from contesting the full Trans-Am schedule, but then again, the Trans-Am didn't have a Drivers' Championship in 1967. (Courtesy Jerry Melton)

Bottom: Canada didn't host a round of the SCCA Trans-Am until 1968. However, Circuit Mont-Tremblant, just north of Montreal, ran an event in May 1967 called Les 4 Heures du Circuit Mont-Tremblant, which featured several local and US Trans-Am A/Sedans. None of the factory teams made the trek, however. With Chrysler having withdrawn support at the end of 1966, Bob Tullius soldiered on as an independent in 1967 in his year-old Dart. His Trans-Am campaign got off to the best possible start when he outlasted all the factory teams to win the Sebring 4-Hour race. Here at Circuit Mont-Tremblant, he finished second to Dick Guldstrand's Camaro. (Courtesy Denis Giguère)

In fact, Ed Leslie and Peter Revson were the only Bud Moore drivers in 1967 to have followed a more traditional sports car racing path. But they soon adopted the combative approach of their team-mates.

While they didn't go out of their way to wreck cars, Bud Moore's guys introduced a new, more aggressive style of driving to the Trans-Am that would set the tone throughout the manufacturer years. Bud Moore was the first to engage top-level drivers specifically for driving, plucking pilots from Ford's extensive war cabinet. This differed to the approach of Shelby American and Penske Racing, whose lead drivers were also full-time employees, building and preparing the cars throughout the week that they raced on the weekend.

In many ways, the addition of Bud Moore Engineering to the Trans-Am in 1967 accelerated the professionalism of the series, through the way the cars were designed and built, the aggressive 'Hail Mary' approach of its drivers, and the commitment to overstepping the many gray areas in the rule book that offered a performance advantage. It all began here.

Dodge Dart

Despite minimal input from the mothership, Chrysler almost won the 1966 SCCA Trans-Am O2 Manufacturers' Championship! But rather than commit itself to the new road racing sedan series, it withdrew what little support it offered and dove further into its stock car and drag racing programs.

However, Ron Grable and Jim Hensel teamed up to build and run a fourth-generation Dodge Dart in selected 1967 Trans-Am races.

Unlike the Mustang, Camaro and Cougar, Dodge designed the Dart to be a dedicated all-rounder, offering several body styles, including four-door sedan, two-door sedan, two-door convertible, and a sporty new two-door hardtop. Although a fresh new design, the '67 Dart shared the same 111in wheelbase as the third-generation model it replaced and, initially at least, most engine options were also carried over, including a pair of Slant-Sixes, and the 273in^3 V8.

Grable entered just two Trans-Am races in 1967: Round eight at Continental Divide where the Dart was disqualified, and Round ten at Riverside where he retired on lap 88 (of 96) with a blown motor. California-based Grable was limited in the amount of travel he could do, so focused largely on SCCA Regional A/Sedan contests.

Interestingly, despite being stripped of his miserly Chrysler support, Bob Tullius and his Group 44 squad ran the full Trans-Am schedule in 1967 with his aging third-generation Dart, the same car he'd raced in 1966.

1967 Trans-Am

The 1967 SCCA Trans-Am was fought across 12 events, kicking off at Daytona International Speedway on 2 February with a dedicated race held the day prior to the annual 24-Hour sports car epic, using the road course layout. Then there was a 4-Hour Sebring contest, followed by races at Green Valley, Lime Rock, Mid-Ohio, Bryar, Marlboro, Continental Divide, Crow's Landing, Riverside, Las Vegas, and Pacific Raceway in Kent, Washington. Teams had the option of using either one or two drivers, and most opted for the former. However, two drivers per car was compulsory in the Marlboro event. Also, Marlboro split the two classes into separate races: U2 on Saturday, O2 on Sunday.

Prize money increased marginally over that of 1966, with $67,550 divvied up over the 12 events to the top ten finishers, and the winner of each class usually netted $1250, with an additional $1000 going to the outright winner.

The Chevrolet fleet, headed by Penske Racing, struggled in the early part of the season, and race wins were mostly split between the Shelby American Mustangs and Bud Moore Cougars. That is, apart from the 300-mile season opener at Daytona. There, the Bud Moore pairing of Dan Gurney and Parnelli

78
44

Opposite, top: Bob Tullius keeps at bay the Camaros of Don Yenko and Craig Fisher, and John Hall's Mustang in Les 4 Heures du Circuit Mont-Tremblant. To the right can be seen the Falcon Sprint of Don Sessler. (Courtesy Denis Giguère)

Opposite, bottom: Although unable to compete with the 1967 factory cars, Tullius was competitive against the latest independent teams, thanks to the impeccable preparation of his Group 44 Dart. Here he leads Don Yenko and Milt Minter in Les 4 Heures du Circuit Mont-Tremblant. (Courtesy Denis Giguère)

Right, top: Peter Revson drove the #15 Cougar at Lime Rock. Here, the BME crew works on the rear end. The Cougar was quite literally a Mustang with an extra 3in on the wheelbase, and decorated in upmarket accessories. It carried all the Mustang mechanical components, including its robust 9in rear end and its drum brakes. All Trans-Am cars in 1967 had drum brakes, even the factory cars. (Courtesy BARC Boys)

Right, bottom: Revson goes for broke on the opening lap of the Lime Rock race, and has already gapped Ron Dykes, Ed Leslie in the second BME Cougar, Craig Fisher's Camaro, and Milt Minter's Mustang. Charlie Rainville can be seen further down the pack in a 1966 Barracuda. Donohue went on to finish second, and Titus third. Both were two laps behind 'Revvie' at the end. (Courtesy BARC Boys)

Jones locked out the front row in qualifying, and while Mark Donohue shot away to an early lead in the Penske Camaro, he soon slowed with fuel pick-up problems resulting from metal filings working through the system from the modified gas tank. With Donohue gone, Gurney assumed the lead until he was forced to stop with a leaking valve cover gasket. Titus then took over until he and Bill Bowman's lapped Porsche clattered into each other and the Mustang pitted to replace a shredded tire. Dick Thompson, driving the second Shelby Mustang (owned by Grady Davis of Gulf Oil) was next to have a turn leading, until his clutch blew. Jones took over but slowed when a rocker arm broke and his motor dropped to seven cylinders.

With all the factory cars tripping up, it was Bob Tullius who seized control in his year-old Dodge Dart, taking everyone by surprise to win after 300 miles. He collected $1000 for winning outright, and another $1500 for the class win, then got home to find a $10,000 check waiting for him from Goodyear Tires. This allowed him not only to run the full 1967 Trans-Am schedule, but also to properly establish the basis for the successes and future growth of Group 44.

98

Opposite, top left: Daytona International Speedway hosted the 1967 Paul Revere 250 on 4 July, using its road course layout. This was not a Trans-Am Championship race, although it was an SCCA-sanctioned event. Both Shelby American and Bud Moore Engineering entered cars. The BME Cougars were driven by Parnelli Jones and Peter Revson. Here the two Cougars rest in the Daytona pits with a pile of American Racing wheels stacked in front of them. Note how the #15 car, usually driven by Jones, has a Firestone decal on the front fender and the #98 car doesn't. Bud Moore was contracted to Firestone, as was Jones, whereas Dan Gurney, who usually drove the 98, was contracted to Goodyear. In the foreground, the various wheels can be seen wrapped in either Goodyear Bluestreak or Firestone Indy tires. (Courtesy Harry Hurst)

Top right: The crew fettles the handsome 98 Cougar, which was driven at Daytona by Revson. He finished sixth, while Jones won the race. (Courtesy Harry Hurst)

Bottom left: The Bud Moore Engineering Cougars were powered by the same 289in^3 small-block Ford V8, topped with a pair of four-barrel Holleys, as the Mustangs. In both cases, they were down on horsepower compared with the larger 302in^3 Camaros. (Courtesy Harry Hurst)

Bottom right: An interesting quirk of the factory Cougars was inclusion of carpet on the floors. This wasn't an FIA Group 2 or SCCA requirement. BME came from a stock car racing background and stock cars tended to use heat mats on the floor to help reduce driver fatigue and limit burning from the exhaust. Perhaps the Cougars used some sort of matting beneath the carpet? It was certainly unique. Note also the factory steering wheel wrapped in padding and electrical tape. This was also common practice in stock car racing. (Courtesy Harry Hurst)

Pace lap for the Bryar Trans-Am, and the Camaro pace car has pulled off the track with the grid about to be launched. Leslie and Revson were handling Cougar duties here, with Leslie sitting on pole, alongside Titus. Rain had started to fall prior to the start. (Courtesy Bill Sutton)

It was a thrilling start to the 1967 Championship, and suddenly, everyone stood up and took notice of the Trans-Am. And the action continued.

Titus took victory in the Sebring 4-Hour, after starting from pole. Bud Moore took three Cougars to Sebring for Jones, Leslie, and Gurney. Leslie finished fifth. Indeed, he was the only Mercury driver to go the full distance. Both Jones and Gurney suffered clutch failure on lap 41!

Mercury scored its breakthrough win in Round three at Green Valley Raceway. In fact, it was better than that – Gurney took the victory from team-mate Jones – and it was a wildly close race between the two FoMoCo heavy hitters. Green Valley featured a sort of Le Mans start. Titus was off the back after barrel rolling his Mustang in practice, and the Shelby team bashed it back into shape with anything heavy and solid they could find. Titus drove right through the field to second position, behind race leader Gurney, until he had to pit from heat exhaustion. Ron Dykes took over Titus' car.

Meanwhile, Jones was ripping back through the field after a slow getaway and caught Gurney at the end. As the pair crossed the line for the last time, Dan took the narrowest of victories; just three feet was in it. Thompson was third in the lead Mustang.

Lime Rock produced more Mercury success. Peter Revson jumped aboard one of the Bud Moore projectiles for the first time and promptly won. Donohue was second while Titus was third. That meant, from the last two races, Mercury scored 18 points to Ford's eight. It was all on!

David Pearson was drafted in for Mid-Ohio, and placed second to Titus. Revson and Leslie were the BME pairing for the Bryar event. Black clouds threatened a good dumping of rain, but the race started dry. Leslie opted to

Left: Donohue and Leslie battle while the wrecked Titus Mustang rests after tangling with the lapped Mustang of Ken Duclos on lap 44. (Courtesy Bill Sutton)

Below: Revson swoops through the Bryar infield in his BME Cougar. After running third behind Leslie and Bert Everett's Porsche in the early stages on a wet track, Revson surged forward when the rain stopped. After Leslie's motor blew on lap 96 (of 156), Revson passed Everett and went on to score another Trans-Am victory for Mercury. (Courtesy Ron Lathrop)

fit wet tires and, while he drifted back in the early laps, on lap 12 everything changed as the deluge began. With that, he surged forward and passed teammate Revson in second, and leader Bert Everett's Porsche, and proceeded to drive away. His motor broke on lap 96 (of 156), however. But Revson was able to save the day for Mercury, hunting down Everett as the track dried, and going on to win by over a lap. Dick Thompson was the lead Mustang driver in third. Donohue broke an axle on lap 93 while Titus had already gone out on lap 44, having collided with the lapped Mustang of Ken Duclos, pirouetting several times, and shortening his rear end by a few feet after hitting the outside banking.

The Marlboro 300 featured the first Trans-Am event where the U2 and O2 classes ran separate races. Both encounters paired two drivers per car. Revson and Leslie drove one of the Bud Moore Cougars, while NASCAR battlers Cale Yarborough and LeeRoy Yarbrough shared the other. Neither car finished. This race was won by Donohue, scoring the first Camaro victory in the Trans-Am.

Leslie was second to Titus at Continental Divide, and Revson was second to Titus at Crow's Landing. Pearson returned for the Riverside race, where he finished first, ahead of Leslie.

By the penultimate race in Las Vegas, the Penske Camaro had the measure of the Ford teams. The 302in^3 Z28 Chevy enjoyed a horsepower advantage over the smaller 289 Fords. However, Chevrolet's stuttering start to the campaign ensured the all-important Manufacturers' Championship would be decided between Ford and Mercury. Donohue won from Bucknum, now driving the Grady Davis Shelby Mustang, while the first Cougar home was that of Jones, in fourth.

For the final round in Kent, Bud Moore excelled, unleashing a third factory Cougar, entered and driven by Allan Moffat, but with full factory support. Gurney and Jones were aboard the two BME cars, while an independent entry was that of Dave Tatum and Bill Pendleton.

Right: Bert Everett's Porsche 911 buzzes past the wrecked Titus Mustang. Had the rain kept falling, Everett would have been hard to beat. Ultimately, he finished second outright at Bryar, and won the U2 class. (Courtesy Bill Sutton)

Below: Allan Moffat gets crossed-up in his Lotus Cortina. He failed to finish the 1967 Bryar race, but at this event the previous year, he drove his Alan Mann Racing Lotus Cortina to an outright victory. That was the second and last time a U2 car won a Trans-Am race outright. As a Ford factory driver, he was given a BME Cougar to peddle in the final four races, to help Mercury in its quest to win the Manufacturers' Championship. (Courtesy Bill Sutton)

Shelby also supported a third car for the final: the customer Mustang of Milt Minter.

The championship contest was tight; Ford held the slimmest of margins, at 62 points over the 61 of Mercury. Whichever manufacturer finished ahead, be it Ford or Mercury, regardless of whether or not Chevrolet won the race, would take home the trophy. Ultimately, Donohue cleared out to win by a lap, but behind him, chaos reigned.

It had been a final of multiple moving parts. The momentum appeared to swing in Mercury's favor when Titus destroyed his Mustang in practice. John McComb had been campaigning a Shelby Mustang customer car all season, which the Shelby team borrowed for the race. They installed whatever salvageable parts they could from the Titus wreck, but didn't change the motor. Things got even better for Mercury when Jones and Moffat qualified second and third behind Donohue.

Minter was the first of the factory cars to drop. He lost oil pressure on lap 11 (of 135). But then Mercury's advantage began to crumble. On lap 59, Jones made a routine pit stop, but his car refused to restart. Meanwhile, Gurney lost time with a slowly deflating tire, and then had to make an extra stop to have the leaking fuel cap refastened. This dropped him down a lap. Moffat was struggling for pace, but then Titus retired the Minter Mustang on lap 65 with a blown engine. If only they'd changed that motor!

While Donohue was untroubled out front, Bucknum found himself promoted to second, despite the Grady Davis Mustang overheating throughout the second half of the race, which had a detrimental effect on his pace. Gurney was scything back through the field, taking chunks of time out of Bucknum. Then a rock flicked up from another car and went through Gurney's windshield, so he was forced to drive with one hand while the other hand held the glass in place.

But the heroics were all to no avail. Gurney was still 40 seconds behind Bucknum's ailing Mustang at the finish, and with that, Ford won the 1967 Trans-Am Manufacturers' Championship.

It had been a season of enormous growth for the Trans-Am. Although the SCCA envisioned the series would mirror European touring car racing, the

Right: Leslie on the charge. He started the race on rain tires, the only factory driver to do so, and shot away to a commanding lead in the early laps. It wasn't to last, however. (Courtesy Bill Sutton)

Below: Pit stop time for Revson on his way to victory. Bud Moore can be seen at the right front of the Cougar. (Courtesy Ron Lathrop)

Left: To the victor, the spoils. Revson enjoys his Bryar victory lap. (Courtesy Bill Sutton)

Below: Ed Leslie gives his team-mate the thumbs-up on his Bryar race win. (Courtesy Ron Lathrop)

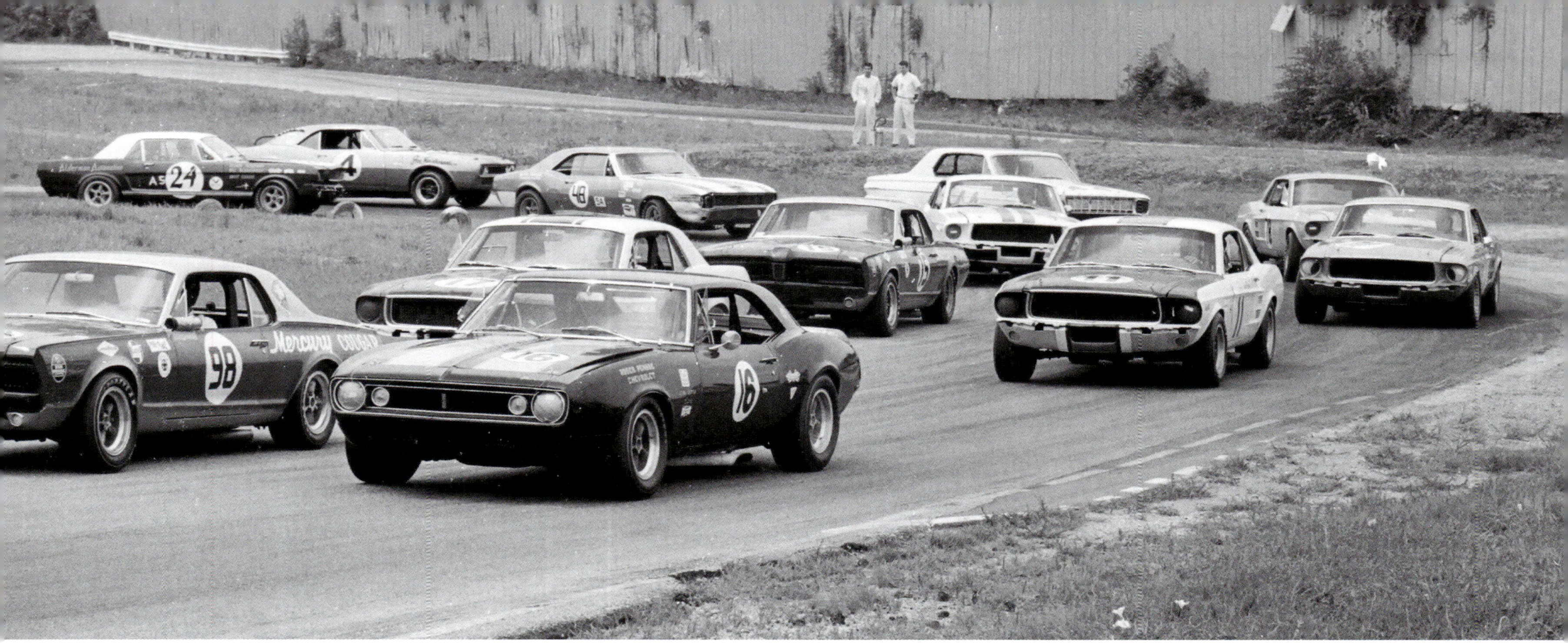
AS 24
4
48
98
Mercury COUGAR
16

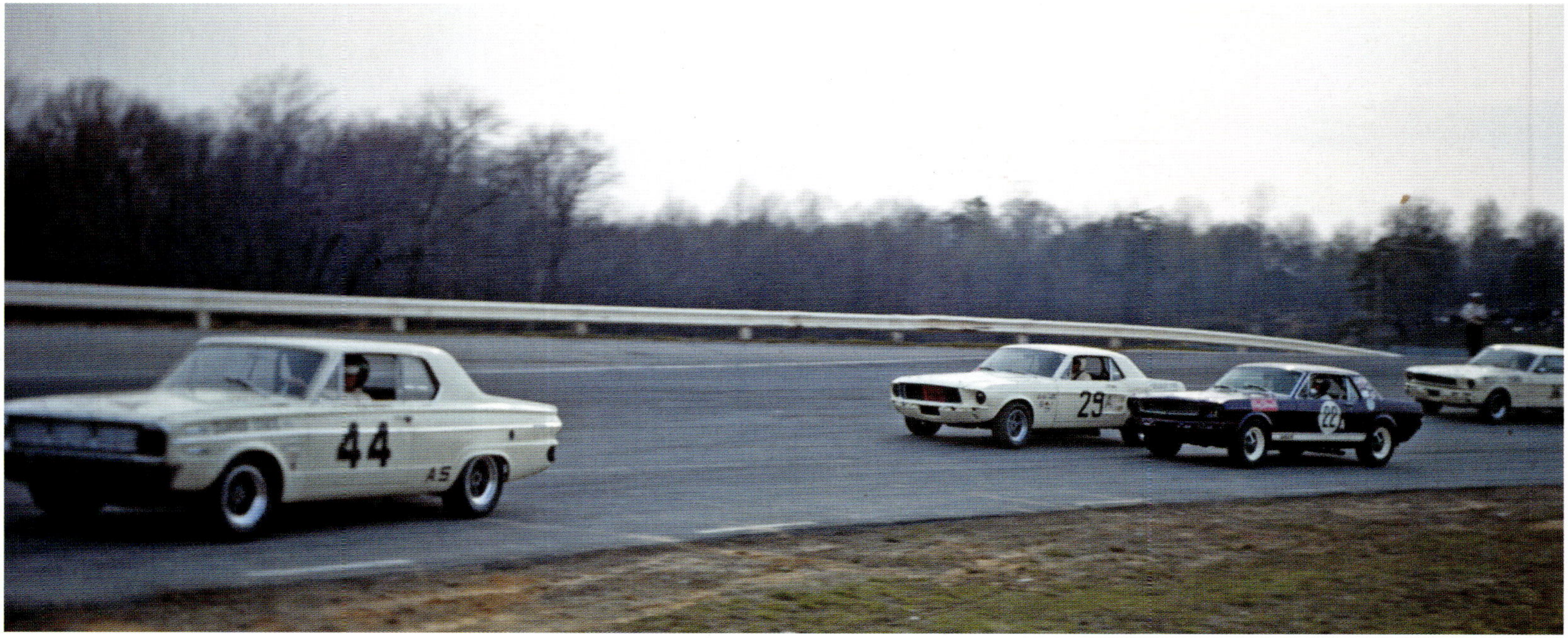
44
AS
29
22

Opposite: The 1967 Marlboro round was the first Trans-Am in which the U2 and O2 cars had separate races. Both included mandatory two-driver entries. The U2 field had its race on Saturday, with the V8s running on Sunday. Only 14 cars contested the O2 race, which was won by Mark Donohue and Craig Fisher in the rejuvenated Penske Camaro. This was the first Trans-Am victory for Chevrolet. The 98 Cougar was shared by Revson and Leslie, while NASCAR stars Cale Yarborough and LeeRoy Yarbrough were in the 15. Neither went the distance. (Courtesy Revs Institute/Duke Q Manor)

Opposite, bottom: Bob Tullius started the Marlboro race from the fourth row of the grid. He shared his Dart with Bruce Jennings. The pair finished fifth, five laps down on the winning Penske Camaro. Giving chase here are the Mustangs of James Sutter/Richard Mandelson (#22), and John McComb/Jim McDaniel. (Courtesy Dave Wiehle)

Pacific Raceways in Kent, Washington, hosted the final round of the 1967 Trans-Am Championship. The two factory Cougars arrive in style on the back of a pair of Ford ramp trucks. (Courtesy Ron Brown)

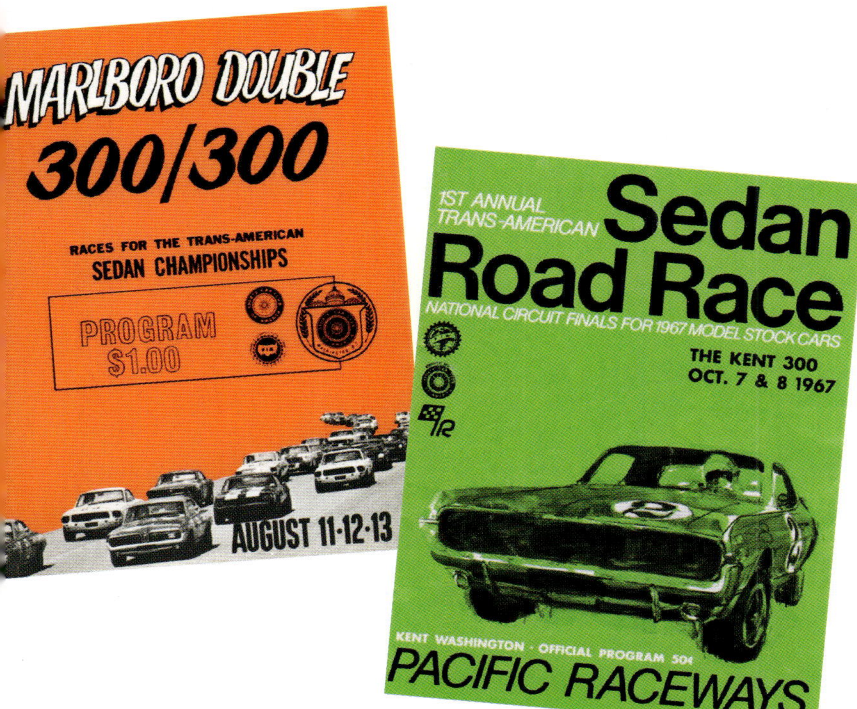

increased involvement of Detroit prompted a notable shift in focus, with the O2 pony cars now grabbing all the headlines. And rightly so. The 1967 Trans-Am had it all: noise, color, drama, and great racing. Also, the addition of drivers like 1963 Indianapolis 500 winner Parnelli Jones and Formula 1 driver Dan Gurney – who won the Belgian Grand Prix in his own Eagle Gurney-Weslake in the same season he drove a Mercury Cougar in the Trans-Am – gave the series enormous credibility. Suddenly, the Trans-Am had come of age.

When the dust finally settled, the overriding feeling at Ford Motor Company was that having two of its brands competing head-to-head was counter-intuitive. Quite fortuitously, and with a little prompting by Ford, NASCAR president Bill France was looking to cash in on the rapidly growing pony car craze. To that end, he established NASCAR Grand Touring, a sort of Trans-Am on speedway ovals, and using much the same regulations. To help his cause, Ford sent Bud Moore and his factory Cougars across to contest the first NASCAR Grand Touring in 1968, leaving the Mustangs to carry on the fight against Ford's real competition, the rival manufacturers, in the Trans-Am.

Far left: Shelby American came to Kent ready to fight. Like the two regular Shelby team cars, a couple of independent drivers were also assist Shelby also outmuscled Bud Moore w this impressive hauler. (Courtesy Ron Brown)

Left: Bud Moore brought two Cougar to Kent for Gurney and Jones, plus a third, entered as an independent, fo FoMoCo-contracted driver Allan Mof And Ed Leslie, seen here leaning on Gurney's Cougar, was also drafted in as a backup driver. Gurney is partiall hidden behind the guy in the grey sh (Courtesy Ron Brown)

Far right: There's that red-carpeted interior again. The BME Cougars ran carpet throughout 1967. From here can also be seen the robust roll cage, which served to stiffen the chassis. This was common practice in NASCAR, but a first in Trans-Am. (Courtesy Ron Brown)

Right: Parnelli Jones, in the race suit, gets ready for battle. His race ended when, after a pit stop, his motor refused to fire. (Courtesy Ron Brown)

Gurney's face says it all: tired, sweaty, dirty, and disappointed. Following delays early in the race, he fought back, but ultimately finished third behind Donohue's winning Camaro, and Ronnie Bucknum's ailing Shelby Mustang. The two points that separated second from third on the road was the difference between winning the Manufacturers' Championship and finishing second. Note the smashed windshield, which Gurney held in place with his right hand to stop it collapsing. It had been a race of drama, but ultimately, Mercury came up short. (Courtesy Ron Brown)

Dan Gurney paces just prior to the start of the Kent Trans-Am, with Jones' Cougar in the foreground. The Trans-Am Manufacturers' Championship all came down to this race. (Courtesy Ron Brown)

The field charges away from the rolling start to begin its 135-lap (303-mile) journey, with the all-important Trans-Am Manufacturers' Championship to be decided. At this moment, with Jones running second and Moffat in third, things were looking good for Mercury. Donohue, who raced away to win easily, was only in it for the glory, with Chevrolet out of the running. (Courtesy Ron Brown)

1968

After two years of employing FIA Group 2 Touring Car regulations to police its Trans-Am fleet, the SCCA decided to throw caution to the wind and go it alone in 1968. This had positive and negative ramifications.

For the SCCA, one of the downsides with Group 2 was that the rules were created for a varied range of cars, with a broad selection of engine sizes, and each make and model effectively had its own set of guidelines based on whatever its manufacturer submitted to the FIA. But, increasingly, momentum in the Trans-Am was swinging toward the 5-liter V8 pony cars produced by Detroit. In this respect, Group 2 was creating more problems than it solved. For example, even though all cars contesting the O2 Manufacturers' Championship were of similar size, wheelbase, engine capacity, and packing around the same power, each had a unique minimum racing weight under Group 2, as submitted by its manufacturer. And there was no stated maximum wheel width. Surely, an even playing field was required to create close racing, and to encourage more manufacturers to join.

The SCCA didn't stray completely from Group 2. For the most part, it just carried out some careful tweaking. The 1968 rules were not greatly different to those of 1967. However, some changes were introduced for O2 class cars designed to be all-encompassing, including a maximum wheel width of 8in (B/Sedans now had a maximum width of 7in, and C/Sedans 6in), and a minimum racing weight of 2800lb.

Engines could now be bored to bring them closer to the maximum 5000cc (305in^3) limit, although factory motors larger than 5000cc were still not allowed to be reduced in size. Also, fenders could now be modified to allow for the increasingly wide tires the manufacturers were producing, although the vehicle profile had to appear stock if viewed from the side.

The rule tweaks were seemingly a smart way forward, particularly with Detroit wading in and waving money about. But not everybody liked the changes. John Bishop wasn't happy. He wanted the SCCA to stick with the FIA regulations, to avoid constant tinkering and interference, particularly by the manufacturers who had a genuine vested interest, but he was overruled so, he quit.

Mercury arrived in 1967 and almost won the championship. But Bud Moore and his team wouldn't get the chance to build on their successes. While they were shuffled across to NASCAR Grand Touring, a new manufacturer arrived in their place to do battle with Ford and Chevrolet: American Motors Corporation (AMC).

The arrival and rampant growth of the Trans-Am coincided neatly with a major restructuring and image rebranding at AMC. It was established in 1954 through the merging of Nash-Kelvinator Corporation and Hudson Motor Car Company. It spent the remainder of the decade producing vehicles that were difficult to fall in love with, but which were cheap to buy and offered great fuel mileage, a niche in which both manufacturers were already well established prior to the merger.

With the big three – General Motors, Ford Motor Company, and Chrysler Corporation – all designing forward-thinking, futuristic, flamboyant land yachts with a baffling array of optional extras, and each locked into expensive annual styling changes, AMC simply focused on what it did best. And during the late 1950s through to the early 1960s, it did appear that the market might swing toward the type of vehicles AMC was producing.

But by the mid-1960s, American Motors was forced to reinvent itself. The American buying public's thirst for excitement and drama (and power) never relented, and AMC needed to adapt, or die. While it continued to serve its loyal customer base with the cheapest, most basic offerings of the big four, it carefully ventured into previously unchartered waters, first with the dramatic Rambler Marlin for 1965, and in late 1967, a two-seat sports car called the AMX, offered as a cheaper alternative to the Corvette. And concurrently came the Javelin, AMC's cheaper alternative to the Mustang ($2490 base price for the AMC versus $2602 for the Ford).

Right: Mercury withdrew from the Trans-Am as a manufacturer in 1968, but a pair of independent Cougars contested the Sebring 12-Hour race, including this example, shared by Billy Hagan, John McVeigh, and Frans Gillebard. Sadly, the engine expired on lap ten. (Courtesy Doug Morton Collection)

Left: For 1968, Mercury was gone. But in its place came the unlikely American Motors Corporation, with its new pony car, the Javelin. Ron Kaplan built the new Trans-Am Javelins, which would be driven by George Follmer and Peter Revson. The team missed the opening race at Daytona, but arrived in style for Round two at Sebring, which for the first time was part of the main 12-Hour race. The bold red, white, blue livery was a stroke of genius. (Courtesy Doug Morton Collection)

Left: The #24 factory Javelin was shared by Peter Revson and Skip Scott. It qualified 24th outright, and completed the full race distance, to finish 12th outright, and fifth in the Trans-Am class. Not a bad way to debut a brand-new car and team. (Courtesy Doug Morton Collection)

Below left: The #26 Javelin was driven at the 1968 Sebring 12-Hour race by Janet Guthrie and Liane Engeman. The pair started in position 68 overall, and while still running at the finish, didn't complete enough laps to be classified. (Courtesy Doug Morton Collection)

And naturally, like any American pony car producer in the late 1960s, American Motors wanted in on the exciting new phenomenon that was the SCCA Trans-Am.

The 1968 SCCA Trans-Am Championship expanded again, to 13 races. However, only the best ten finishes would count. Furthermore, the first two races at Daytona and Sebring were now part of the main event, rather than a standalone race the day before that nobody watched, although the U2 grid had its own Saturday race at Sebring. Nearly two months after Sebring came War Bonnet, followed by Lime Rock, Mid-Ohio, Bridgehampton, Meadowdale, Circuit Mont-Tremblant in Quebec (1968 was the first year

Lime Rock Park hosted Round four of the 1968 Trans-Am, and the Ron Kaplan factory Javelin team was proving its impressive debut at Sebring was no fluke. Follmer finished second in Round three at War Bonnet, while Revson in the #3 qualified on the front row at Lime Rock, alongside Mark Donohue's dominant Penske Camaro. On the second row are the Shelby Racing Co factory Mustangs, which changed color every race during the early 1968 rounds. On row three can be seen the white Camaro of Craig Fisher. (Courtesy Don Feeley)

Moments after the start and Donohue is already surging ahead. He'd go on to win by two laps from Jerry Titus in the first Shelby Mustang, and Revson. (Courtesy Don Feeley)

Right: A dramatic action shot of Revson powering his Javelin around Lime Rock, on his way to third position. Note the body damage. Banging fenders was fast becoming a regular thing in the Trans-Am. (Courtesy BARC Boys)

A Javelin crew member throws water over the rear deck during a pit stop to dissipate the fuel spillage which all teams experienced. Revson was the only AMC driver to start the Lime Rock race after Follmer's motor blew in the morning warm-up and the team didn't have time to swap in a replacement. (Courtesy BARC Boys)

the Trans-Am visited Canada), Bryar, Watkins Glen, Continental Divide, Riverside, and finally, Pacific Raceway in Kent, Washington, on 6 October.

AMC Javelin

The AMC Javelin dropped perfectly into the pony car dimensional format established by the Mustang. It sported a 109in wheelbase (1in longer than the Mustang), a unique body style that wasn't shared with AMC's more mundane offerings, an affordable base price, and a long list of optional upgrades, including a selection of in-line six and V8 motors. The biggest engine available initially was a 343in^3 V8, but a 390 arrived in mid-1968. The entry-level V8 was a 290, which formed the basis for AMC's entry into the Trans-Am. The sporty option package from which the Javelin was homologated was called the SST.

Mustang buyers could choose from three body styles, while the Camaro was available in either coupe or convertible form. But Javelin buyers had to make do with just the standard fastback body style. However, it was a great-looking car, and quite sporty.

Roy Chapin Jr was promoted to chairman of AMC in 1967, and was determined the Javelin should go racing. A competition committee was headed up under Vic Ravioli and Carl Chakmakian, and a full factory-funded Trans-Am program was approved.

Some within the industry expected Bob Tullius and Group 44 to be assigned the job of building and racing the factory Javelins, but Ravioli and Chakmakian brought in Jim Jeffords to oversee the operation instead. Jeffords had a background in marketing and was a former racer himself, having campaigned, with great success, a purple Corvette called the 'Purple People Eater' to a brace of SCCA B/Production sports car championships. Jeffords then appointed engineer Ron Kaplan to build and run the cars.

Kaplan, who'd previously prepared race cars for Nickey Chevrolet, took some convincing. He quickly identified that AMC lacked the required engineering support and the Javelin was missing the aftermarket homologated parts for Kaplan and his small crew to compete on even terms with the might of Ford and Chevrolet. He took some coaxing, but eventually agreed.

George Follmer and Peter Revson were hired to drive the two Javelins. Jeffords, meanwhile, teamed up with the AMC marketing department and concocted a brilliant, bold paint livery for the cars, of red, white, and blue, in large vertical stripes, with great big numbers on the doors, and Javelin lettering emblazoned down the rear quarters. As well as being wildly patriotic, these were also the AMC corporate colors. It was a stroke of genius, and would be carried across to all of AMC's racing programs. But they also had a little fun with it by reversing the liveries; the number 3 Javelin featured a red nose and blue rump. The number 4 was the opposite.

The 1968 factory Javelins weren't just frilly showboats. For its part, AMC assisted Kaplan as much as it could, and listed on the Javelin homologation sheet an adjustable rear-deck wing held aloft by a pair of end plates, among other parts to help the cause. Carl Chakmakian in particular bent over backwards to assist Kaplan and ran requested components through the system as dealer-installed options, to appease the SCCA.

Kaplan sent a batch of 290in^3 motors to Traco Engineering, headed by Jim Travers and Frank Coon. Traco was one of the best in the business, and built, among others, the engines for Penske Racing. Traco went right through the

JAVELIN
3
JAVELIN
4
CARS
31

Opposite: Bridgehampton produced another front-row start for Revson. Team-mate Follmer shared the second row with new Penske Racing recruit Sam Posey. The two Shelby Racing Co Mustangs were on row three. (Courtesy Revs Institute/Duke Q Manor)

Far left: The AMC factory team arrives at Meadowdale with its pair of Javelins. It made for an impressive sight. (Courtesy Greg and Mike Long)

Bottom left: Aside from the two factory Javelins, this independent entry appeared early in the weekend at the Meadowdale Trans-Am. However, it didn't actually start the race. The large stock car number on the door and bodywork signage suggests this might be a NASCAR Grand Touring car, taking in a little Trans-Am action when the series came to town. (Courtesy Greg and Mike Long)

Above: By 1968, all the factory Trans-Am teams were building tall fuel towers, Kaplan's crew included. (Courtesy Greg and Mike Long)

Left: The Trans-Am offered a great way for manufacturers to show off products to an enthusiastic audience, and American Motors was quick to take advantage. This spectacular AMX was displayed at Meadowdale, and was also used as the pace car. (Courtesy Greg and Mike Long)

Above left: American Motors was the official course car at the 1968 Meadowdale Trans-Am, and AMC sent a fleet of street Javelins to make sure it was well represented. (Courtesy Greg and Mike Long)

Above: The Kaplan AMC hauler offered a great viewing platform during the Meadowdale race. Note the stack of wheels and Goodyear Bluestreaks ready to be bolted on the two factory Javelins during their stops. The Javelins, like all the factory teams in 1968, used magnesium American Racing Torq Thrust wheels. (Courtesy Greg and Mike Long)

Left: Meadowdale marked the debut Trans-Am race for the first Pontiac Firebird in the series. Driven by Craig Fisher, the Firebird was a former Penske Racing Camaro, fitted with Firebird body parts. Despite this little disagreement with a fence during practice, the Firebird was bashed back into shape for the race, and Fisher finished fourth behind winner Donohue, plus Revson and Posey. (Courtesy Greg and Mike Long)

The Javelin team arrives at Circuit Mont-Tremblant, in Canada, for Round eight of the 1968 Trans-Am. (Courtesy Denis Giguère)

AMC units, which were bored to 304in³. Kaplan designed some neat details, including a low-mounted alternator to help lower the center of gravity, and a flat-bottom oil pan featuring valleys and trapdoors to prevent the bearings being starved of lubricant. Backing the AMC 304 was a heavy-duty Borg-Warner T10 four-speed transmission.

The Javelins missed the opening race at Daytona but made Round two at Sebring. However, they were down on power compared with the other factory cars. The Traco-built AMC motors featured an Edelbrock intake manifold with a single four-barrel Holley mounted on top. Ford and Chevrolet were using special manifolds that carried two four-barrel carburetors, and these were shown to improve horsepower and torque. There were limited options for the AMC unit, so Kaplan had Edelbrock manufacture a cross-ram intake manifold to his own design, on which were mounted two 600cfm four-barrel Holleys. Chakmakian ran it through the American Motors system, and included it on the Javelin homologation sheet, where it was approved for use from 1 May. After that, the factory Javelins were never wanting for power compared with the Fords and Chevys.

Kaplan's Javelins used Kelsey-Hayes disc brakes, front and rear, which Chakmakian listed as a dealer option. Adjustable Monroe shocks were fitted front and rear, and the front geometry was similar to that of the Mustang. The rear-end design featured track bars and roll bars and a transverse Panhard rod, with various fabricated brackets and towers holding everything in place.

The Kaplan-built Javelins rolled on magnesium American Racing Torq-Thrust five-spoke wheels. The Javelin homologation sheet also listed a small chin spoiler and, somewhat audaciously, the Craig Breedlove roof spoiler. However, while the chin spoiler made it onto the race cars, the roof spoiler didn't.

PETE
REVSON
GOODYEAR
CHAMPION

Clockwise from far left: Peter Revson and George Follmer, looking like cool dudes in their AMC attire. American Motors sold a lot of Javelins off the back of the performances this pairing produced in 1968. (Courtesy Denis Giguère)

Resting in the Circuit Mont-Tremblant pits. Rattle guns for changing wheels during pit stops was a relatively new concept in 1968, and massively reduced stop times. (Courtesy Denis Giguère)

Follmer's Javelin goes through tech inspection at Circuit Mont-Tremblant. The pit garages and pit lane can be seen in the background. The garages had mini grandstands on top of them. (Courtesy Denis Giguère)

Revson shared the front row at Circuit Mont-Tremblant with Donohue, while Posey and Follmer started on row two. (Courtesy Denis Giguère)

Pontiac Firebird

A fourth Over 2 marque entered the Trans-Am in 1968: Pontiac Firebird. However, this was an independent effort, not one supported by Pontiac.

The Pontiac program was instigated by Canadian businessman Terry Godsall, who'd previously partnered with Roger Penske on the Camaro. There were rumors Godsall may be elected to run the AMC Javelin operation, but this came to nothing.

The Firebird made its debut in Round seven of the 1968 Trans-Am at Meadowdale, with the brilliant but incredibly shy Craig Fisher at the wheel. Fisher, a fellow Canadian, already enjoyed a close relationship with Godsall, and therefore, with Penske Racing. He partnered with Mark Donohue in the 1967 Marlboro event to give Camaro its first Trans-Am race victory.

On debut, Fisher qualified Godsall's Firebird ninth, and surged forward in the race to finish fourth. It was an encouraging start. Only, the Firebird wasn't what it appeared to be.

Godsall had lofty ambitions. Indeed, his father ran the TEREX company, which supplied components to General Motors, and having worked with Penske, he wanted to snag himself a factory deal. Pontiac was the logical answer.

Pontiac first launched the new Firebird on 23 February 1967. It was, in almost every sense, an upmarket Camaro in much the same way the Mercury Cougar was an upmarket Mustang. But unlike the Cougar, the Firebird shared the Camaro's 108in wheelbase. The Firebird sported a handsome quad-headlight nose with wraparound chrome bumper integrated into the design. There were faux vents in the rear quarters, and Pontiac's traditional quartet of slatted tail lights.

Under the surface the Firebird was offered with a pair of Pontiac in-line six motors, and four V8s – two 326in³ and two 400in³. And therein lay the problem. Although the Firebird was just a fancy Camaro, it didn't have a suitable engine for the Trans-Am. Both its V8s were larger than 5000cc, and SCCA regulations didn't allow engines to be reduced in size.

But Godsall was smarter than that. He somehow convinced the SCCA that in Canada, the Firebird could be special-ordered with a 302in³ Z28 Chevy engine. It's unclear whether anyone at the SCCA believed him, but it didn't matter. Perhaps the SCCA didn't view Godsall as a genuine threat. Or, more likely, it just wanted another manufacturer on the grid.

And so it was that the Pontiac Firebird that Fisher raced to fourth place at Meadowdale was powered by a Chevy motor. And to further muddy the waters, it wasn't a Firebird at all: it was a Camaro. A Penske Camaro, no less.

Penske Racing had introduced its new and improved 'lightweight' Z-28 at the Crow's Landing round of the 1967 Trans-Am. It featured a heavily acid-dipped bodyshell, and Donohue drove it to victory in the last two races that season. He then partnered with Craig Fisher in this car to finish third outright at the 1968 Sebring 12-Hours event, which doubled as Round two of the Trans-Am Championship.

Penske Racing constructed two new Camaros for the 1968 Trans-Am, and when the second of these was completed after Sebring (the first 1968 car debuted at Daytona), the 1967 lightweight was surplus to requirements. Therefore, Penske sold the car to Terry Godsall. It was painted white with a black hood, and wore signage from Gagnon Spring, a Canadian spring manufacturer owned by Bob Gagnon. Fisher debuted it in Round four of the Trans-Am at Lime Rock, as a Camaro. The team missed the next two races at Mid-Ohio and Bridgehampton, before rolling into Meadowdale with the Camaro now sporting Firebird bodywork.

The Fisher Firebird received a few changes beneath the skin, most notably a Pontiac ten-bolt rear end in place of the Chevy 12-bolt. Also, Godsall chose to have the brilliant Al Bartz prepare the Z-28 Chevy engines, instead of Traco.

Making a Camaro into a Firebird isn't as difficult as it sounds, because all the front panels are interchangeable. The only cutting and welding required was for the slats in the rear quarters and, of course, the tail pan. The Camaro and Firebird shared the same front and rear spoilers.

Follmer laps Rusty Jowett's independent Camaro at Circuit Mont-Tremblant. (Courtesy Denis Giguère)

Follmer was nothing if not spectacular in his fight for third with Posey. (Courtesy Denis Giguère)

Throughout the second half of the season, Fisher produced some stirring performances, and even got on the podium a couple of times. And then, at the final race in Kent, a second yellow Firebird joined the fleet, driven by 'Mr. Trans-Am', Jerry Titus.

Titus had been a cornerstone of Shelby's Trans-Am success. He was a trained musician before switching careers, becoming an automotive mechanic, then a motoring journalist. He wrote for *Sports Car Graphic*, and from there began amateur racing in the late 1950s. His achievements brought him to the attention of Carroll Shelby, which prompted another career change.

The Titus/Shelby partnership had delivered an abundance of success, including winning the coveted 1965 SCCA American Road Race of Champions in the B/Production sports car division with the Shelby GT350. Titus sealed the 1966 Trans-Am Manufacturers' Championship for Ford with his victory (and only appearance of the season) in the final race at Riverside. He then spearheaded the 1967 Shelby Trans-Am program with the Mustang, bringing Ford its second successive championship.

JAVELIN
3

Opposite, inset: Revson impressed again, and took the battle to Donohue in Canada. If not for being clobbered by Dick Bauer while lapping him, Revson would have likely finished second. Instead, his team-mate took the spot, after finally getting the better of Posey. (Courtesy Denis Giguère)

Opposite, main: Craig Fisher worked his way through the pack at Circuit Mont-Tremblant in the Firebird after starting down the order. He finished fourth. (Courtesy Denis Giguère)

Above: Ron Kaplan, pictured in the Bryar pits, tending to one of his Javelins. (Courtesy Ron Lathrop)

Right: Follmer's office, complete with ample seat padding. (Courtesy Ron Lathrop)

But the 1968 Trans-Am had been a tough year for Shelby, and for Titus. To bridge the horsepower gap to Chevrolet, Ford fitted its 302in^3 motor fitted with tunnel-port cylinder heads. They were a concept first tried, with great success, on Ford's NASCAR Grand National stock car program. But the demands placed on a big-block engine swooping around a speedway oval and held in a near-constant high-rpm range are quite different to those of a small-block in a road-racing environment. The tunnel-port 302s blew themselves to pieces with alarming regularity.

Outside of Mark Donohue at Penske Racing, Jerry Titus was almost certainly the most sought-after driver on the Trans-Am grid, and Pontiac approached him about heading up its ambitions to run a Trans-Am program

Top: The factory Javelins used Traco-built motors bored to 304in^3. An Edelbrock cross-ram intake manifold carried a pair of four-barrel Holley carburetors. (Courtesy Ron Lathrop)

Above: With the hood opened on the Craig Fisher, its Camaro origins can be seen. Car owner Terry Godsall convinced the SCCA the Firebird could be ordered in Canada with a Z28 Chevy motor, which of course it couldn't. Regardless, the SCCA approved Godsall's request, and the converted Penske Camaro raced on as a Chevy-powered Firebird, complete with GM cross-ram intake manifold. (Courtesy Ron Lathrop)

In the Bryar Trans-Am race, Follmer ran strongly to finish second to Donohue, albeit four laps behind. But nobody got near Donohue and the flying Penske Camaro for much of the 1968 Trans-Am. (Courtesy Bill Sutton)

in 1969. Prior to the final race at Pacific Raceway, Carroll Shelby got wind of the fact his star driver was talking to another manufacturer, and the pair promptly parted ways.

With Titus needing a car for the Kent race, he approached independent Camaro owner/driver Jon Ward, who'd just finished fourth in the previous event at Riverside, incidentally, one spot behind Fisher. Terry Godsall reportedly bought Ward's Camaro, which was quickly lashed together with the required Firebird bodywork changes, in much the same way as Fisher's car.

Titus only went and put it on pole! He led the first third of the race before the Bartz-built Chevy popped on lap 43 (of 135). It wasn't quite the result he was hoping for, but for Titus, with team ownership and a Pontiac factory contract in his back pocket, a new chapter was about to begin.

1968 Trans-Am

With the AMC program having started late, the Javelins missed Daytona. But three cars arrived for Sebring. George Follmer shared the number 25 Javelin with Jerry Grant, while Peter Revson was with Skip Scott in the number 24. With this being an FIA international race, the Javelins couldn't wear the numbers 3 and 4 that they would for the rest of the season. The third Javelin, number 26, was officially entered by G&H Engineering. It was driven by

Above, left: While his team-mate finished second at Bryar, Revson went out on lap 37 (of 125) with a blown motor. (Courtesy Bill Sutton)

Above: When Fisher's Firebird showed up for the Bryar race, it was sporting a jazzy new paint scheme of yellow with black scallops. Fisher failed to finish the Bryar race. (Courtesy Bill Sutton)

Left: Flag marshals watch from the safety of their infield 'hump' while Follmer cranks out another lap on his way to second position in the Bryar race. (Courtesy Bill Sutton)

female racers Janet Guthrie and Liane Engeman, from the Netherlands. The Follmer car qualified fastest of the three, in 20th position outright, and fifth in the Trans-Am class, behind the two Penske Camaros, Smokey Yunick's beautiful black and gold Camaro (driven by Al Unser and Lloyd Ruby), and the lead Shelby Mustang. It was an impressive showing, given the second

The 1968 Trans-Am Championship concluded at Pacific raceway, in Kent, Washington. The big news was that Shelby Racing and Jerry Titus had parted ways. Titus arrived at Kent with this rough and tough-looking Firebird, an expansion of the Terry Godsall team. Like the Craig Fisher Firebird, this car started life as a 1967 Camaro, originally built by Jon Ward. It was hurriedly rehashed as a Firebird for Titus to race here. (Courtesy Kevin Skinner)

More big news. The brilliant Peter Revson had been relieved of his duties after the Riverside race, and his place at Kent in the factory AMC squad was filled by Lothar Motschenbacher. (Courtesy Kevin Skinner)

This attractive Mercury Cougar was the creation of Dave Tatum, a former Kar-Kraft consultant who, in 1967, was working for Burien Lincoln-Mercury. Tatum convinced the dealership owner an entry into the Trans-Am would be beneficial, for promotional purposes. With Mercury in a tight battle with Ford for the 1967 Manufacturers' Championship, this car was constructed as a semi-factory effort to help in Mercury's bid to win the title. Tatum himself did the driving. (Courtesy Kevin Skinner)

Shelby Mustang started two places further back. The Revson Javelin lined up in grid 24, while Guthrie/Engeman were back in position 68, from 87 starters.

Come the race and the Follmer/Grant Javelin blew its engine on lap 90, but Revson and Scott raced their way to 12th outright, and fifth in class. Guthrie and Engeman endured a few spicy encounters, which included Engeman supposedly causing a Porsche 911 to spin right in front of the JW Automotive Ford GT40 driven by Paul Hawkins through the Esses, which Hawkins duly hit. The tough Australian straight-shooter didn't mince his words when being interviewed on national television. "The Porsche didn't cause the accident," he lamented. "Those bloody birds did." Of course, the interviewer pushed Hawkins for more details, and after venting his side of the story, he finished with, "Those bloody birds shouldn't be in the race. A woman's place is in the bedroom or the kitchen, and if she can't cook, send her back to the bedroom." Janet Guthrie, in particular, was an accomplished racer and pioneer who would go on to enjoy a career competing in Indycar and NASCAR.

Follmer's Javelin rests in the pits. The damage on the front likely came from punting a slower car during practice. (Courtesy Kevin Skinner)

The speed of the factory Trans-Am cars, combined with the professionalism of their teams, took many in the sports car racing world by surprise at Daytona and Sebring, further showcasing just how good this championship had become. Jerry Titus and Ron Bucknum finished fourth outright at Daytona in their Shelby Mustang, headed only by a trio of factory Porsche 907 prototypes. And then at Sebring, Penske Racing went one better with Donohue and Craig Fisher, when they finished third outright, behind a pair of Porsche 907s. A lowly American stock-block sedan finishing on the podium at one of the world's most prestigious sports car races! That can't be right, can it?

Round three of the Trans-Am Championship was held at War Bonnett. This was the first race the Kaplan Javelins ran with their new Edelbrock cross-ram intake manifolds with dual Holleys, and Follmer in particular was competitive with Donohue in the Penske Camaro, and the two Shelby Mustangs of Titus and Parnelli Jones, who was making a rare 1968 Trans-Am appearance. This quartet pulled away from the pack to engage in their own little fight, until Jones spent two laps in the pits, and Titus smoked the first of several tunnel-port heads. Independent Mustang racer Malcolm Starr crashed on lap 63. Four spectators were injured and the race was stopped. When it resumed, Donohue was able to pull a gap to Follmer, and went on to win by 40 seconds from Follmer, while a recovering Jones was third, and Revson fourth in the second Javelin.

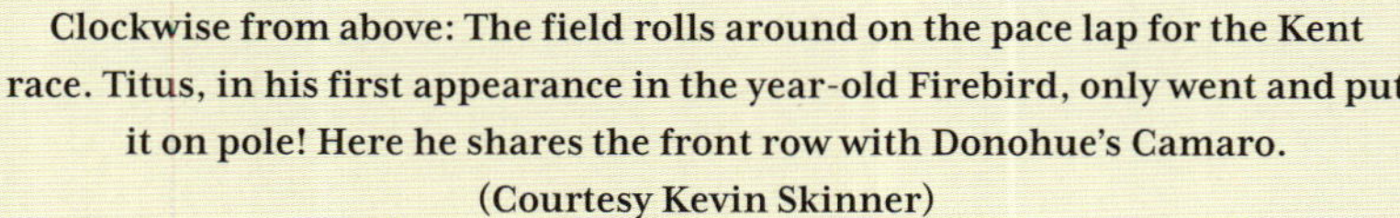

Clockwise from above: The field rolls around on the pace lap for the Kent race. Titus, in his first appearance in the year-old Firebird, only went and put it on pole! Here he shares the front row with Donohue's Camaro. (Courtesy Kevin Skinner)

Behind Titus and Donohue can be seen the two Shelby Mustangs of Horst Kwech and Revson (who bounced back quickly following his AMC marching orders), the two factory Javelins, while Craig Fisher's Firebird shares the fourth row with Tony Settember's Camaro. (Courtesy Kevin Skinner)

Lap one of the Kent race, and Donohue jumped out to an early lead. But the determined Titus would soon get past. (Courtesy Kevin Skinner)

Above: Settember's Camaro leads Fisher and Motschenbacher early in the race. (Courtesy Kevin Skinner)

Top: Fisher gradually worked his way through the field in the second Firebird. (Courtesy Kevin Skinner)

Above: Dale Mahar entered the Kent Trans-Am in his charismatic old 1966 Plymouth Barracuda. He qualified 25th from 26 cars, including the U2 entries, and lasted five laps before mechanical failure ended his day. (Courtesy Kevin Skinner)

Top: Motschenbacher was a regular Can-Am sports car racer, so it took him some time to settle into his new role aboard the Javelin. He ran well but ultimately retired on lap 46. (Courtesy Kevin Skinner)

Above: Follmer had a race of adventure in the Kent event. He battled among the leaders in the early laps before smacking into the rear of Kwech's Mustang, resulting in several laps in the pits while the damaged sheet metal was cut away. He still finished, however, in seventh, 19 laps down on the winner. (Courtesy Kevin Skinner)

Top: Titus' fairytale debut aboard the Firebird came to a smoky end when the Chevy motor blew itself to pieces on lap 43. To that point he'd offered Donohue one of his biggest challenges of the season. Naturally, Donohue cruised to another victory. (Courtesy Kevin Skinner)

Above: A mid-pack battle between Tatum and Bob Barker's 1967 Mustang. The Cougar retired on lap 66, while Barker went on to place ninth, from ten finishers. (Courtesy Kevin Skinner)

Second and third place for the 1968 Kent Trans-Am. Fisher worked his way through the pack and, as the big guns faltered, popped out in second position at the end. After the motor blew in the sister Firebird, Titus switched roles and helped change tires during one of Fisher's stops. Ron Bucknum finished third in his year-old Mustang. (Courtesy Kevin Skinner)

Donohue won again at Lime Rock, by a full two laps! The Penske juggernaut was in a league of its own for much of the 1968 Trans-Am. Everyone else was fighting for second. At Lime Rock, it was Titus who finished second, while Revson was third. This pairing came to blows on the track, with Revson protesting against Titus for rough driving, for which the Ford driver was fined. Follmer needn't have shown up. His Javelin blew its motor in the morning warm-up and couldn't be replaced in time for the race.

At the Mid-Ohio event, AMC crew member and part-time amateur driver John Martin stepped in for Follmer, who was at Mosport in Canada, racing an Indycar. And Martin surprised everyone, including himself, possibly, by sticking it on pole! However, there was more to the story. Donohue was also competing at the Mosport Indycar race, and missed Trans-Am qualifying on Saturday. He flew to Mid-Ohio, jumped aboard the Penske Camaro, and started off the rear of the grid. By lap ten he was leading, and went on to finish a lap ahead of Titus, while Revson was third. Martin retired ten laps before the finish with engine troubles.

Just 19 cars started the Bridgehampton race, and now Penske Racing had two Camaros, which was bad news for everyone else. Sam Posey would be Donohue's team-mate for four races. Revson was impressive here. He started on the front row alongside Donohue (Posey and Follmer were on row two), and was the only driver to stay within striking distance of flying blue Camaro. However, the Javelin's gearbox cried enough at two-thirds distance. This promoted Posey to second, briefly, until a tire went flat and he had to pit. This promoted Follmer to second, which is where he finished.

Meadowdale was the debut of the first Pontiac Firebird in the Trans-Am. This was, of course, Craig Fisher's converted Camaro. Fisher finished fourth, behind winner Donohue, and one position behind Posey. Revson split the two Penske cars by placing second. Follmer suffered road rage and crashed into a lapped Mustang that got in his way, and was promptly disqualified.

At Circuit Mont-Tremblant, it was Follmer's turn to split the Penske Camaros. Fisher again finished fourth. Revson was running second to Donohue early in the race until Volvo driver Dick Bauer went clattering into him while being lapped.

In the next race at Bryar, Fisher's Firebird arrived sporting a groovy yellow paint scheme with black scallops. Donohue won here from Follmer, by four laps! However, the race was quite entertaining, as the two factory Shelby Mustangs held the top two positions early on. Horst Kwech was driving alongside Titus. Both struck trouble; Kwech blew a motor and Titus broke an axle. The Shelby crew swapped in a replacement, and he finished tenth. Also, Tony Adamowicz, driving an Under 2 class Porsche, was keeping Donohue honest on the tight Bryar track, but he blew a tire. He still finished third. Both Fisher and Revson retired.

So dominant was Donohue and the Penske team that, even running as a one-car program for a portion of the season, the Over 2 Manufacturers' Championship went to Chevrolet, with four races remaining.

At the Watkins Glen race, the two Penske Camaros locked out the front row of the grid, with the two Shelby Mustangs on row two, and the two factory Javelins on row three. Donohue was ill, so Posey took the reins and led much of the race until flat-spotting a tire while trying to avoid the lapped Camaro of Rusty Jowett, who spun in front of him. Posey pitted for a replacement, which promoted Titus to the lead. Mercifully, the Mustang's engine held together to the end. Posey was second, and Donohue third.

Amazingly, this was the first race since the season opener at Daytona that Donohue didn't win. Also, it was the first race since Sebring that at least one of the Javelin drivers wasn't on the podium. Revson was fourth at Watkins Glen.

Donohue was back to his winning ways at Continental Divide. He won by two laps from Craig Fisher, completing the first podium finish for Pontiac in the Trans-Am. John McComb, in an independent Mustang, was third. Dan Gurney was brought in to drive the second Shelby Mustang, but even he couldn't keep the tunnel-port 302 from blowing itself to pieces. Titus' race ended the same way. Follmer finished down in tenth after various delays, while Revson went off course and was disqualified for receiving a push start.

Only 18 cars started the Continental Divide race, but that number swelled to 32 for the next event at Riverside. Donohue was on pole, but his Camaro suffered a rare engine failure. Titus made it as far as lap 15 in what would be his last ever race with Shelby. In the end, Kwech's tunnel-port motor went the distance, and he won by nine seconds from Revson. Fisher was third in the Firebird. Follmer was another to have a motor let go.

And so it was that Titus and Shelby parted company between the Riverside and Kent races. But also, Jim Jeffords and Peter Revson got into a fight, and Jeffords fired Revson, replacing him with Lothar Motschenbacher. Revson wasn't out of work for long – he took Titus' seat at Shelby.

Just how good was Jerry Titus? In a two-year old independent Camaro fitted with some Firebird body panels, he took pole position in Kent, toppling the dominant Mark Donohue Penske Camaro. Had his motor held together for 135 laps, he might just have won the race, too. He was leading Donohue when he went out.

Heading into the Kent race, Ford and AMC were in a close fight for second in the Manufacturers' Championship. Come the race, the factory Mustangs and Javelins duked it out. Eventually, Follmer bulldozed Kwech, which eliminated the Mustang, but also damaged the Javelin, requiring Follmer to spend several laps in the pits while the team carried out repairs. Follmer was later fined for his driving. Then, Revson's Mustang broke an engine. That put AMC in the driving seat. Until mechanical failure eliminated Motschenbacher's Javelin. Although Follmer was circulating at the finish, he was 29 laps behind winner Donohue, and out of the points. In the end it was Ron Bucknum with his independent Mustang who saved the day for Ford, despite being eight laps down on Donohue when he finished.

There were no race wins for American Motors and Pontiac, but in 1968, pickings were slim for everyone who wasn't Mark Donohue.

In the end, Chevrolet won the 1968 Trans-Am Manufacturers' Championship at a canter, with 90 points. Ford was a distant second on 59, while the new kids, American Motors, were third. From 13 races, the Penske Camaro won ten of them.

For American Motors Corp, the Trans-Am hit a home run for Javelin sales. Roy Chapin publicly announced, at Javelin's launch in late 1967, that the company was aiming for a sales target of 35,000 units in its first 12 months. All told, AMC sold just over 55,000 Javelins in 1968. And the sight of Follmer and Revson punching out regular podium finishes in their patriotic red/white/blue Trans-Am racers no doubt played a significant role in that success, and in providing AMC's pony car with almost instant credibility among buyers.

But furthermore, AMC introduced the Javelin (and AMX) as part of a rebranding shake-up, and to help attract a more youthful buyer than its traditional customers who were on average, aged 40. That, too, proved a success. The average age of Javelin buyers was 29. The Javelin showed that pony cars, and the Trans-Am, were good for business.

When AMC entered the Trans-Am, many considered it a bit of a joke. After all, the company was best known for producing underpowered, stodgy economy cars, not aspirational sports cars, and certainly not race cars! But by the end of the year, the only one laughing was AMC.

By the end of 1968, any manufacturer with a pony car in its line-up needed to be in the Trans-Am. In just three years, it had blossomed beyond all expectations, and was now one of the most hotly contested championships on the planet.

1969

Throughout the short history of the SCCA Trans-Am series to this point, Ford Motor Company and the Mustang had been a constant. Ford won the Manufacturers' Championship in 1966 and 1967, but was soundly beaten by Chevrolet in 1968.

Ford doubled down on its efforts for 1969 to knock Chevrolet off its perch. Bud Moore returned to the Trans-Am stable to run a pair of new Boss 302 Mustang Sportsroofs alongside Shelby. Between them, BME and Shelby would field four cars at each event, sometimes five. These were designed and built (some fully, some partially) by Kar-Kraft, which had been instrumental in Ford's colossal GT40/GT MkII/GT MkIV Le Mans program. With the company having achieved its Le Mans objectives in 1967, it had no hesitation in moving Kar-Kraft over to the Trans-Am Mustang project, such was the level the series was operating at. This put Ford's rivals on notice.

Given the way the points system worked, if Mustangs filled the first four positions at each race, the Trans-Am Manufacturers' Championship would be done and dusted with half the season still to run.

Of the four factory Mustangs, the two Bud Moore Engineering cars would be driven by Parnelli Jones and George Follmer, while Peter Revson and Horst Kwech, for the most part, were assigned to Shelby.

Chevrolet would enter two cars at every event for the first time, with Ron Bucknum joining Penske Racing to support Mark Donohue.

After its encouraging 1968 debut, which yielded no race wins but enormously positive reviews, American Motors Corporation returned with another two-car program, directed by Ron Kaplan Engineering.

Pontiac now competed as a fully-fledged factory effort, running a two-car team for the full schedule.

The SCCA changed little in the Trans-Am regulations to that of 1968, other than increasing the minimum weight slightly to 2900lb. Also, front and rear bumpers were a requirement for the first time.

The 1969 Trans-Am Championship was reduced from 13 rounds to 12, and the season-opening long-distance races at Daytona and Sebring were also removed from the schedule. The series had grown to such an extent that it no longer needed propping up by way of inclusion in the Daytona and Sebring enduros. However, there remained a pair of sedan classes at both events: T5.0 (touring cars up to 5000cc) and T2.0.

An interesting new recruit for the factory Javelin team was John Martin. He had been an amateur racer who was also a crew member on the Javelin team in 1968. His one-off appearance in the 1968 Mid-Ohio Tran-Am, where he subbed for Follmer and put the car on pole, no doubt helped in his promotion. (Courtesy Ron Lathrop)

Left: Having jumped aboard the Jon Ward Camaro (which became a Firebird) in the final round of the 1968 Trans-Am, and put the car on pole, Jerry Titus and Ward teamed up in the same car, now painted an attractive red and white hue, and entered the 1969 Daytona 24 Hours. The Trans-Am series no longer included Daytona in its schedule, so this was a non-championship outing for Titus and Ward. Regardless, not only did they win their T5.0 class (touring cars up to 5000cc), they finished third outright, beaten only by a pair of Lola T70 prototype sports cars. (Courtesy Will Day (static daylight photo) and Harry Hurst (night-time racing))

Traditionally, the first two Trans-Am races kicked off at Daytona and Sebring in February and March, respectively. From there followed the regular Trans-Am schedule which began at Green Valley Raceway in April 1967, and War Bonnet Park in May 1968. Because the two international endurance epics were missing from the 1969 Trans-Am calendar, so the championship finally began at Michigan International Speedway on 11 May. It concluded at Riverside on 5 October.

In many ways, even though it lacked participation from Chrysler, the 1969 Trans-Am was the most competitive season ever. There were, at each race, ten factory cars: four Mustangs, two Camaros, two Javelins, and two Firebirds. Cheating was rife. The Ford and Chevy teams, in particular, were truly pushing the boundaries in just about every area. Essentially, if the rules didn't specifically say you couldn't do something, the factory teams just assumed you could. And even then they lived in the gray areas, where tiny fractions of performance could be extracted.

SCCA tech officials were kept on their toes. The factory teams were cheating, but doing so in such a manner that indiscretions were often hard to detect, if at all. Indeed, stock examples of the Mustang, Camaro, Javelin and Firebird traveled with the series and were used as reference points because the factory teams were manipulating everything from body shapes to engine placement.

With the cars all being so close on track, Penske Racing looked at opportunities to reduce pit stop times by working with sponsor Sunoco Oil to concoct a monstrous 20ft fuel tower that would dump 22 gallons (the maximum fuel tank size in 1969) into the back of a Penske Camaro in just a few seconds. Naturally, everyone was protesting against everyone else, and the SCCA was trying to stay on top of it all – and largely failing.

In many ways, the factory AMC and Pontiac squads struggled to keep pace, but for different reasons. That said, neither enjoyed the funding of the Ford teams and Penske Racing. And ultimately, all 12 races would be won by the Fords and Chevys, with AMC and Pontiac left to pick up the scraps. But even though Ron Kaplan's Javelins showed strongly in 1968, it was the new kid, Pontiac, which looked more likely to steal a win in 1969.

Pontiac Firebird

Jerry Titus had ambitions loftier than that of being a paid driver. He wanted to run his own factory team, and in Terry Godsall he found the ideal partner. Titus and Godsall founded T/G Racing (Titus/Godsall) to run the 1969 Pontiac Trans-Am program. Titus would drive one of the cars, naturally. Surprisingly, Craig Fisher was not in the second seat. Instead, Milt Minter was.

For its part, Pontiac offered an optional handling package for the Firebird, featuring various performance components and trim pieces to be carried across to the race cars, including a special hood with two broad functional intake snorkels, a rear wing that held aloft the deck lid by a pair of end plates, and faux fender vents which could very easily be made functional to allow engine bay heat to escape.

In a brazen move, Pontiac approached the SCCA to acquire the use of the name Trans-Am on its optional handling package, to which the SCCA agreed. For $1083, Firebird buyers could order the Trans-Am Performance And Appearance Package, and Pontiac paid the SCCA $5 for every unit sold. Although Pontiac's tenure in the Trans-Am as a factory squad would ultimately be relatively brief, it continued to use the Trans-Am name for its top-of-the-line Firebird street car, and pay the SCCA for the privilege, until the model was canceled in 2002. It was an agreement that worked well for both parties.

The Trans-Am Performance And Appearance Package consisted of white paint with two metallic blue stripes stretching down the center to a blue tail. The T/G race cars would wear much the same livery, although it evolved somewhat as the season progressed.

Al Bartz built the motors for T/G Racing, as he had done with the independent Fisher and Titus Chevy-powered Firebirds in 1968. The initial plan was to use Pontiac units with special tunnel-port cylinder heads, known as the Ram-Air V. These were 400in^3 lumps de-stroked to 303in^3. The SCCA didn't allow engines larger than 5000cc to be reduced in size, but evidently, Pontiac had plans to produce the Ram-Air V in the requisite numbers. Or maybe it didn't. Shelby ran 302in^3 motors in 1968 fitted with tunnel-port heads and these were very much not a production option, but the SCCA allowed them anyway. Would the SCCA turn a blind eye to the de-stroked Pontiac motors? In the end, it didn't matter.

The stock Pontiac 400 motor sported a 4.125in bore, and 3.75in stroke. Bartz installed a 2.83in crank to achieve 303in^3, which came in just nicely within the 305in^3 maximum limit. Bartz also trialed at least one block with lowered deck height.

Meanwhile, the little T/G Racing crew got to work building cars for the upcoming season. Titus wooed some pretty smart cookies for the Firebird project, including Herb Adams and Jerry Schwartz. On the surface, and given it had bought the rights for the name Trans-Am, the Pontiac program looked financially healthy, but in fact, T/G Racing was operating on possibly the smallest budget of all the factory teams. So, to make ends meet, it opted to build and field its own cars, and also construct a small number of race-ready

Left: Another new recruit at AMC was Ron Grable. Grable can be seen barreling around the banking at Michigan International Speedway during the opening round of the 1969 Trans-Am. From this angle can be seen the pronounced hood bulge that appeared on the 1969 Javelins, which caused some consternation. (Courtesy Ron Lathrop)

Below: Grable splashes his way around another lap of the convoluted MIS road course. Having started off the rear of the grid, he quickly surged forward before retiring on lap 52, exactly at the halfway point. Note how big the fender flares were on the 1969 factory Javelins compared with the '68 models. Like all the 1969 factory teams, the Javelins rolled on eight-spoke Minilite wheels. (Courtesy Ron Lathrop)

Top: Ron Kaplan's team arrived at MIS with three Javelins, including this 1968 model, driven by Bob Tullius. Tullius rewarded the team with a fighting fourth place finish, the best result for any of the AMC entries. (Courtesy Ron Lathrop)

Above: Jerry Titus presses on in his factory T/G Racing Firebird, which made its competition debut here at MIS. The Firebirds were supposed to run Pontiac power, but when the team reverted to Chevy units, so the SCCA required the cars be retrofitted with 1968 front sheet metal and rear spoilers. It was a strange demand, and did nothing for the Firebird's otherwise handsome aesthetics. For whatever reason, T/G Racing chose not to fit front chin spoilers to the cars at MIS. The front-end lift here is evident. (Courtesy Ron Lathrop)

Top: Making its way around the MIS banking is one of several 1969 Firebird customer cars built by T/G Racing. This particular Firebird was the Ortega Equador Racing example driven by Guillermo Ortega. It appears that Ortega leased the Firebird from T/G Racing just for this event. (Courtesy Ron Lathrop)

Above: The Hol-Arc team out of Texas was another to run a T/G Racing Firebird in the 1969 Trans-Am. In fact, it had two of them. The attractive metallic blue racers sported a reversal of the T/G color scheme. The #72 car was driven in the season opener by Brad Dunn and Larry Harley, seen here battling with Tullius. (Courtesy Ron Lathrop)

Top: Another of the Firebirds; albeit, a 1968 model. This is Richard (Dick) Brown, in the same car raced in the 1968 Trans-Am by Craig Fisher, that being the former Penske Racing Camaro. (Courtesy Ron Lathrop)

Above: A fourth AMC Javelin contesting the opening Trans-Am at Michigan International Speedway was the that of Ted Roberts, which he shared with Dick Guldstrand. This was a former 1968 Ron Kaplan-built factory car. (Courtesy Ron Lathrop)

Battle of the Firebirds. Dick Brown and Milt Minter go at it on the MIS banking. Minter was the second driver of the T/G Racing factory team, although it's not clear why his car was painted an unflattering brown and yellow at this event. It's possible another team planned to buy or lease it. Either way, Minter retired on lap 71 (of 104). (Courtesy Ron Lathrop)

The Dunn/Harley Firebird fights over the minor places with Rusty Jowett's Camaro. In the end, the Firebird got home just in front, in sixth, one place ahead of Jowett, who drove his car solo. (Courtesy Ron Lathrop)

Firebirds to sell to independent teams. T/G would retain three of the cars; two for drivers Titus and Minter, plus a spare. At least three others would be sold. Although this replenished the coffers somewhat, it placed enormous strain on the crew, who had to build three times as many cars as everyone else.

Regardless, the handsome new T/G Firebirds bristled with several innovations, and some of the most beautiful fabrication work on the Trans-Am grid. The roll cages were made from chrome-moly, and neatly connected the front subframe pickup points. The beefy rear end combined a Bonneville center section and smaller Tempest outer tubes, plus a Watts-link, and carried a differential oil cooler.

Herb Adams was Pontiac Special Projects lead engineer, and was perhaps best known for creating the Ram-Air induction system, by making functional the cosmetic twin-snorkel hood scoops on the GTO and Firebird. But he was also a clever chassis and suspension guy and was ushered in to help design the T/G Firebird Trans-Am race cars.

Because the Trans-Am had evolved into a brutal combat sport where body contact was a regular thing, the T/G Firebirds featured special front bodywork that could be quickly removed and replaced as a single unit.

Early pre-season testing had the Firebirds rolling on the latest American Racing 200-S 'daisy' wheels. But as with most factory Trans-Am teams in 1969, by the time they rolled into Michigan International Speedway for the first event, they were wearing eight-spoke Minilites.

T/G Racing took an interesting approach to housing the increasingly chunky rear tires being used on Trans-Am cars. Rather than flaring the wheel openings, it instead made a careful cut around the circumference of the rear quarter, then pulled it out by a couple of inches at the tail, added in a metal section, then gradually filled the gap tapering toward the rear of the doors.

It was all looking so promising for T/G Racing and Pontiac, until things started to unravel just before the season began. The Ram-Air V motors were proving difficult to develop, with the main bearings being starved of oil due to their surface speed. Remember, dry-sump units weren't allowed in the Trans-Am. Yet. With more time, a solution could be found. But time was scarce. To that end, a request was put to the SCCA that the team power its cars with Chevy motors, as it had done in 1968. This was granted, but on the basis they be fitted with 1968 Firebird front bodywork, and small rear deck spoiler. It was a strange demand, and overnight the handsome Pontiacs were transformed into grisly Frankenstein monsters.

But because T/G Racing was building and preparing so many cars for 1969, including customer cars, this meant fitting all of them with Chevy powerplants and retrofitting all of them with 1968 bodywork. And with that, the team was already on the back foot before the season had even begun.

T/G Racing was a little haphazard initially, with Titus throwing himself into the role of car builder alongside his crew, while nobody was there to oversee the direction of the team. Terry Godsall remained in Canada and wasn't part of the day-to-day running of the program. Partway through the season, Titus convinced Walt Hane to join and take on an organizational role. Hane was himself an engineer, and former driver. He'd won the 1966 SCCA Road Race Of Champions in B/Production aboard a Shelby GT350, then became a Trans-Am tech inspector for the SCCA, so he knew all the tricks.

When Hane arrived at T/G Racing, he helped knock the team into shape, and Titus and Minter enjoyed some strong results in the back half of the season. However, the team was based in Tarzana, California, while Hane lived in Colorado. He camped at a motel in Tarzana during his tenure at T/G Racing, before moving on at the end of the season, to be replaced by Lew Spencer, who'd worked for Shelby until that team was discontinued at the end of 1969.

AMC Javelin

Ron Kaplan's factory AMC Javelins were the surprise package of the 1968 Trans-Am. Everyone had been impressed by Kaplan's achievements, having so quickly developed the Javelin into a genuine Trans-Am contender against the might of Ford and Chevrolet. In the capable hands of George Follmer and Peter Revson, the striking red, white and blue pairing scorched to several podium finishes in 1968, and Kaplan was expected to build on that momentum in 1969 and maybe even snatch a race win or two.

But in many ways, the factory AMC Javelin program went backwards in 1969. Or maybe the competition just progressed faster. Firstly, Kaplan decided to build the motors in-house, and spent a lot of time developing special blocks with lowered decks, along with custom rods, pistons, and crankshafts. This resulted in a pretty strong unit with good power, but it was time-consuming.

Kaplan didn't have the technical support from American Motors that Penske did with Chevrolet and that the Ford teams enjoyed. The 1969 factory Javelin drivers struggled to perform with cars that suffered from a lot of understeer, and Kaplan and his crew didn't seem to have an answer.

As for the pilots, Follmer and Revson were hired by Ford, and replaced by young amateur driver Ron Grable, and John Martin, who'd been one of Kaplan's crew members in 1968. It seemed an odd choice given how much the competition had stepped up its game. Both did the best they could with what they had, but the program appeared to be in some disarray. Grable

It had been a rough lead-in to the 1969 Trans-Am Championship for the little T/G Racing team. Despite switching engine brands, swapping out sheet metal, and building at least six cars, Jerry Titus rewarded his crew with a podium finish at MIS, behind Parnelli Jones and Mark Donohue. In the tricky wet conditions, the brilliant Titus led the race for a while, until a shredded tire forced an unplanned pit stop. Still, it was an encouraging start to the season. (Courtesy Ron Lathrop)

performed pretty well, while Martin was gone by mid-season, and his seat was filled by a variety of drivers including Lothar Motschenbacher and Jerry Grant.

Because of his desire to develop engines in-house, the program was delayed, and in fact, Kaplan wanted to skip the 1969 season altogether and use the time to test and develop, to come back stronger in 1970. Kaplan's plan was to test at each track straight after the Trans-Am series had raced there. But the bigwigs at AMC were having none of it.

Although they struggled against the other factory cars, the 1969 Javelins were good-looking machines. They had neatly flared front and rear fenders to house the latest magnesium Minilite wheels and the latest fat Goodyear tires. They arrived at the first race at Michigan International Speedway sporting huge fiberglass hood bulges to house Edelbrock tall-ram intake manifolds carrying a pair of Holley Dominator four-barrel carburetors. The hood bulges weren't actually available on the Javelin street cars, so AMC produced 1000 of them and mailed them to Javelin customers!

Alongside the two new 1969 factory Javelins, Kaplan also prepared and entered a 1968 car, which contested several events. Bob Tullius drove it in the opening race at Michigan, where the two '69 models arrived so late, they missed qualifying. Kaplan had to gain special permission to start them off

The Ted Roberts Javelin makes a pit stop for a new set of Goodyears on its way to ninth place. (Courtesy Ron Lathrop)

Opposite: A picture tells a thousand words. The Tullius Javelin speeds around the MIS banking on its way to an excellent fourth place, while the sister car of Martin stopped on lap 46 with a failed universal joint. (Courtesy Ron Lathrop)

the back of the grid. It rained during the early part of the race, and Grable in particular went well, sprinting right through the field to reach fourth, before the motor broke. Martin had already retired by that stage when the driveshaft fell out.

In the end, Tullius brought home the old 1968 car in fourth. This would equal the best result of the season for the team.

According to Kaplan, the SCCA told him he couldn't return with the special low-deck motors he ran at Michigan. After Michigan, the Javelins never looked to be in the hunt.

Aside from the factory cars, Ted Roberts campaigned a privateer Javelin in the 1969 Trans-Am. This was one of the former 1968 factory cars, and Roberts ran almost the full 1969 schedule.

Just before the end of the 1969 Trans-Am, Roger Penske announced he and American Motors Corporation had agreed a three-year deal to run the factory Trans-Am Javelins.

1969 Trans-Am

There were 12 rounds making up the 1969 Trans-Am Championship, kicking off at Michigan International Speedway on a strange makeshift course using parts of the banked oval, parts of the infield, and a section of the car park! That was followed by more traditional circuits at Lime Rock, Mid-Ohio, Bridgehampton, Donnybrooke, Bryar, Circuit Mont-Tremblant, Watkins Glen, Laguna Seca, Seattle, Sears Point, and finally, Riverside. Chevrolet and Ford won all of them. Pontiac and AMC were shut out completely.

As if the Michigan race needed to be even more chaotic than its quirky track layout dictated, it rained! The Bud Moore Mustangs were fastest, but the wet conditions, countless crashes and shunts, multiple pit stops to switch between wet and dry tires, plus people losing time getting stuck in the mud, guaranteed an unpredictable outcome. And certainly, that proved to be the case. Mark Donohue was declared the winner, but four hours after his victory celebration, it emerged that Parnelli Jones actually won for Bud Moore.

For a time, Jerry Titus assumed the lead and controlled the race. But a tire blowout ended his chances, and he finished third behind the belatedly

demoted Donohue. Tullius was next in Kaplan's year-old Javelin. Minter failed to finish in the second factory Firebird.

Three of the T/G Racing customer Firebirds also attended the Michigan race. The Hol-Arc Racing Team, based in Texas, ran two of them, driven by Richard McDaniel and Brad Dunn. They were painted an attractive metallic blue with white stripes, essentially a reversal of the factory cars. Bill Ortega drove the third T/G customer Firebird, which was finished in a curiously unflattering two-tone brown and yellow. Dunn, sharing his car with Larry Harley, placed fifth at Michigan. Ortega finished 13th and wasn't seen again. He wound up one spot back from Canadian Dick Brown, driving the Firebird Craig Fisher raced in 1968 for Terry Godsall, that being, the 1967 Penske Racing lightweight Camaro.

1969 17: Dick Brown, on his way to 12th. (Courtesy Ron Lathrop)

With the factory Javelins going out, it was up to the independents to fly the AMC flag, and aside from Tullius, Ted Roberts started his 1969 campaign with a ninth-place finish. His former 1968 factory Javelin was shared with the legendary Chevrolet tuner, Dick Guldstrand.

For Round two of the championship at Lime Rock, Ron Hunter took over the '68 Kaplan Javelin raced by Bob Tullius at Michigan, and campaigned it in most of the races that followed. He finished ninth there, and indeed, was the best placed of the four Javelins. Grable finished, but was struck by multiple delays, ultimately being classified in 20th, and the last car still circulating. Martin retired in the other factory Javelin, as did Roberts in the other independent Javelin.

Minter was best placed of the Firebird contingent, in fifth. McDaniel and Brown were 17th and 18th. Titus and Dunn retired.

The Lime Rock Trans-Am clashed with the Indianapolis 500, and as such, most of the big names were missing. Because there was only a Manufacturers' Championship in 1969, and no drivers' championship, the clash didn't actually matter, and in the end, it was a Mustang one-two finish, with supersubs Sam Posey, driving for Shelby, who took the win from Swede Savage, who was filling in at Bud Moore Engineering.

The crazy, twisting and undulating Mid-Ohio Sports Car Course produced a titanic battle between Donohue and Jones for the win, but neither was in front at the finish. They pummeled their equipment so badly that both ultimately suffered delays while their cars underwent repairs. In the end, Bucknum took victory for Penske.

Grable got to enjoy a rare finish. He emerged in fifth. Roberts was ninth, one position behind Larry Harley in one of the Hol-Arc Firebirds. Titus and Minter were circulating at the end, but well down the order after several unscheduled stops. Martin went out with steering failure.

Bridgehampton produced a better result for Titus. He was third behind Follmer and Donohue. Minter was back in 16th at the end. Both the factory Javelins retired (Martin with engine failure, Grable from an accident), but Roberts finished sixth in his independent Javelin, and scored a single point for struggling AMC.

Titus produced another encouraging performance at Donnybrooke. He

'Hey Javelin.' (Courtesy Ron Lathrop)

Below: That's better! Milt Minter, on his way to fifth at Lime Rock, with his Firebird wearing the same white and blue livery (and not brown and yellow) as team-mate Titus. (Courtesy BARC Boys)

Above: The T/G Racing and Hol-Arc Firebirds assemble in the Mid-Ohio pits. Note how the T/G cars have the extra section added in the rear quarters to allow for the latest wide tires. (Courtesy Ron Lathrop)

Right: Javelin team driver helmets. (Courtesy Ron Lathrop)

The pace lap for the 1969 Mid-Ohio Trans-Am, with arch-enemies Parnelli Jones and Mark Donohue sharing the front row. (Courtesy Ron Lathrop)

Clockwise from left: Mired in the mid-pack are the Minter Firebird and Roberts Javelin. (Courtesy Ron Lathrop)

Grable works his way through the numerous U2 Porsches, while looming up quickly in the background is one of the Shelby factory Mustangs. (Courtesy Ron Lathrop)

Titus qualified an encouraging third at Mid-Ohio, but suffered various delays during the race, and ultimately finished 19th, 15 laps down on race winner Ron Bucknum in the second Penske Camaro. The winding, undulating track layout ensured plenty of panel damage as the fast cars spent the day fighting through lapped cars. (Courtesy Ron Lathrop)

Larry Harley gets out in the dirt in the Hol-Arc Firebird as a Bud Moore Mustang dives down the inside. Harley started eighth at Mid-Ohio, but dropped down to 17th at the finish. (Courtesy Ron Lathrop)

Grable started the Mid-Ohio race in 11th, but worked his way to fifth at the end. (Courtesy Ron Lathrop)

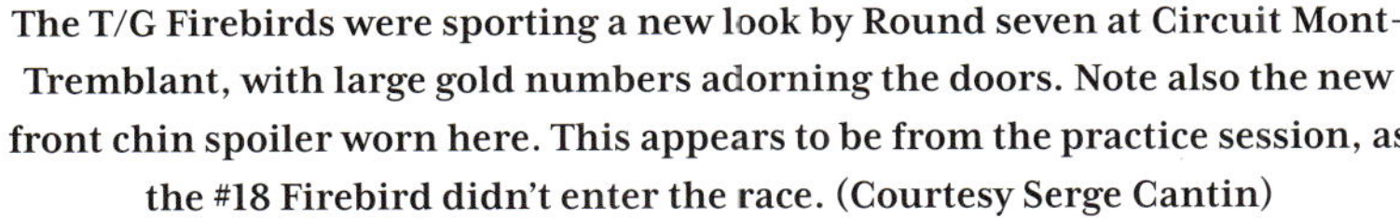

The T/G Firebirds were sporting a new look by Round seven at Circuit Mont-Tremblant, with large gold numbers adorning the doors. Note also the new front chin spoiler worn here. This appears to be from the practice session, as the #18 Firebird didn't enter the race. (Courtesy Serge Cantin)

Titus running laps in the #13 Firebird during practice at Circuit Mont-Tremblant. Note how his car is wearing five-spoke American Racing 200-S 'daisy' wheels here. The T/G cars wore these wheels early in the year before switching to Minilites for the first race. (Courtesy Gord Reilly)

was fourth, behind Jones, David Leslie – who was subbing for an injured Bucknum – and Revson. Titus benefited from the retirements of pole man Follmer, who was leading when he and a lapped Mustang ran into each other, and Donohue, who suffered engine failure. Ted Roberts was again the best placed Javelin driver in sixth and, again, the two factory Javelins retired.

The Penske pairing took a one-two finish at Bryar, from Revson and Follmer. Titus was fifth, after being outqualified by Bob Tullius. Tullius arrived at Bryar as a spectator, but ended up making a single appearance in the second factory Firebird. He ultimately went out with engine failure. However, the impressive Dick Brown was just one position behind Titus at the finish. Vic Campbell was having a turn in one of the Hol-Arc Firebirds, and was the last classified driver, in 11th, after various delays.

Again, the two factory Javelins failed to finish. Actually, Grable failed to start. He crashed in practice and repairs couldn't be completed in time for the race. Ted Roberts, who'd been the AMC savior the last few races, also retired after a wheel-mounting issue.

For the next race at Circuit Mont-Tremblant in Canada, Lothar Motschenbacher was aboard the second factory Javelin, with Martin and the team having parted company. And, while Vic Campbell was making his second appearance in one of the Hol-Arc Firebirds, Indycar legend Johnny Rutherford was in the other.

Meanwhile, Dick Brown found himself aboard one of the latest 1969 T/G Firebirds in the Canadian race when Jerry Titus damaged Brown's car while testing it a few days before the event.

This was the race that unraveled Ford's efforts to reclaim the Trans-Am Manufacturers' Championship. George Follmer took pole and was running second to Donohue early in the race when, on lap 14, his Boss 302 blew its motor to pieces and laid down an oil slick, from which he himself spun. Within seconds he was joined by Revson, Kwech, Grable, Vic Campbell, Tony Adamowicz (Porsche 911), and Ed Wachs (Alfa GTA), with wrecked cars literally stacked on top of each other. The race had to be red-flagged. In a single incident, three of the factory Mustangs suffered massive damage, and Ford spent the rest of the season trying to recover.

When the race restarted, Donohue drove away from a somewhat depleted field to win from Titus and Leslie. Motschenbacher scored the equal-best result of the season for the factory Javelin team in fourth. Rutherford retired the second Hol-Arc Firebird on lap 56 of 97, while Roberts and Brown were also retirees.

Watkins Glen followed just one week later. The Ford teams and Kar-Kraft managed to cobble together three working Mustangs from all the wrecks for Jones, Follmer, and Revson, with Kwech missing out.

Donohue won this race from arch-rival Jones, while independent racer Rusty Jowett filled the final podium position in a Camaro. Craig Fisher was next, in another Camaro, followed by Ron Grable, who had his best result of the season. Indeed, both factory Javelins went the full distance. Sports car racer Gordon Dewar was in the second car, and finished tenth.

Neither T/G Firebird finished. Titus didn't even complete the first tour before he dropped out with a sizable oil leak. Team-mate Minter suffered the same fate, and was a spectator on lap 13. Neither Johnny Rutherford nor Dick Brown reached the finish in their Firebirds. The Hol-Arc team was now down to one car after the pile-up in Canada.

The Trans-Am headed cross-country to the West Coast for the final four races of the 1969 season, and Titus and Grable both qualified strongly at Laguna Seca, in fourth and sixth. However, the Firebird pilot retired with a broken throttle linkage, and Grable suffered various delays to wind up in 13th.

Milt Minter had a good day, and was fifth behind winner Donohue, Leslie, Gurney (driving Horst Kwech's repaired Shelby Mustang) and Revson. Jerry Grant was two spots further back, having a turn in the second factory Javelin. And two spots further back from Grant was future Javelin factory driver Roy Woods, making his Trans-Am debut in a Camaro.

The Kent 300 at Seattle International Raceway netted Jerry Titus a solid

Top right: Dick Brown found himself aboard one of the latest 1969 T/G Firebirds for the Canadian Trans-Am race. His car suffered damage while being tested by Titus earlier in the week. The attractive orange with black scallops paint scheme somewhat replicated that of his earlier Firebird. Brown always produced great-looking race cars. He failed to finish here. (Courtesy Gord Reilly)

Right: The Circuit Mont-Tremblant Trans-Am was one of high drama, high attrition, and enormous carnage. The Titus Firebird got its nose punched in but still finished the race. Indeed, Titus was second at the end. (Courtesy Serge Cantin)

The big field rumbles down the hill at Laguna Seca for Round nine of the 1969 Trans-Am. The Bud Moore Mustangs bolted on a set of sticky Firestones in qualifying and locked out the front row, while the impressive Titus shares row two with Donohue's Camaro. (Courtesy Ron Brown)

third place behind the returning Ron Bucknum in the Penske Camaro, and Parnelli Jones. Minter finished seventh. An interesting addition to the Kent race was Bill Pendelton's elderly Mercury Cougar, which was eighth. Both Ron Kaplan Javelins blew their motors.

At Sears Point, Shelby brought a Mustang for Gurney to drive, but Gurney didn't show up. Rumor had it he and Ford were at loggerheads, and that Gurney was in negotiations with Chrysler for a possible Trans-Am program in 1970.

Donohue won Sears Point after Jones controlled the race for 69 of 80 laps. Follmer was third, and Titus fourth. The T/G Racing owner/driver was now enjoying regular results at the pointy end of the field with Walt Hane having joined the team and knocking it into shape. Indeed, Titus finished one place ahead of Bucknum in the second Penske Camaro, and Minter was right behind Bucknum. Progress indeed!

Both factory Javelins finished the Sears Point race, in eighth and ninth. Neither Ron Hunter nor Ted Roberts went the distance in their independent Javelins, while none of the independent Firebirds traveled west.

Riverside hosted the final round of the 1969 SCCA Trans-Am, and Penske Racing arrived safe in the knowledge it had wrapped up the Manufacturers' Championship for Chevrolet. In spite of this, there were five factory Mustangs, with Bud Moore bringing a third car for Indycar star Al Unser to drive

Titus enjoyed another strong event, qualifying fifth behind Jones, Donohue, Follmer and Revson, and alongside Bucknum. On the next row was Unser and Jerry Grant, going well in the lead factory Javelin.

Top: The third row of the Laguna Seca race featured Ed Leslie in the Penske Camaro, and Grable in the lead Javelin. (Courtesy Ron Brown)

Above: The two Javelins running together at Laguna Seca. John Martin was dismissed following the Bryar race, and his place was filled by a handful of different drivers, including Lothar Motschenbacher, and here at Laguna Seca, Jerry Grant. (Courtesy Ron Brown)

Top: Titus went on to finish fifth at Laguna Seca, four laps down on winner Donohue. (Courtesy Ron Brown)

Above: Grant started off the back of the grid after a practice shunt, but drove steadily through the field to finish seventh. (Courtesy Raynald Bélanger Collection)

Far left: After his strong qualifying performance, Grable had a tough race at Laguna Seca, and eventually finished 13th following several delays. His day was only marginally better than that of Parnelli Jones, whose failing, flaming rear end can be seen catching fire here. (Courtesy Doug Dodd)

Left: Battle of the minor places. Ron Hunter, aboard the Kaplan 1968 Javelin, chases the John Wilkins Mustang and Don Zacharie Porsche into the Corkscrew. (Courtesy Doug Dodd)

Bottom left: Through the rolling hills, the field heads around the pace lap for the Kent Trans-Am at Pacific Raceways. The first five rows included Donohue, Jones, Follmer, Titus, Revson, Gurney, Bucknum, Jowett, Grant, and Settember. (Courtesy Kevin Skinner)

Come the race and Jones and Donohue set off out front, as they had all season. Then Jones ran into the back of the Penske Camaro and spun. He was convinced Donohue had brake-tested him, so waited a lap for his rival to come into view, then promptly jumped out in front of him. Donohue hit him hard in the rear and spun. Jones drove his crumpled, smoking Mustang back to the pits, climbed out, and stormed away. Donohue recovered, but Follmer was now in the lead.

Follmer looked to have the race in the bag until one of his wheels broke. Frustrated, he decided to drive back to the pits, with a shower of sparks emanating from the exposed brake disc, and when he went to stop, the Mustang veered hard into the pit wall. Unser had already retired with a blown engine, so that was three Bud Moore Mustangs out.

Donohue went on to win from Bucknum, while Titus collected another

Further back in the pack was Dick Brown in the orange Firebird, alongside Roy Woods, Ted Roberts and Ron Hunter in the Javelins, and Jerry Gregory's Camaro. (Courtesy Kevin Skinner)

Far left: 1969 was the last season the O2 and U2 cars ran together in the same race. In 1970, the U2 cars had their own Saturday contest at each event. (Courtesy Kevin Skinner)

Left: Lap one in the Kent race and Jones leads out to lead Donohue, Follmer, and Titus. (Courtesy Kevin Skinner)

Bottom left: Revson can be seen here leading Bucknum, Jowett, and Grant. Jowett was a particularly impressive independent driver. (Courtesy Kevin Skinner)

Right: Titus had another good day in the Firebird at Pacific Raceways. He finished third behind winner Bucknum, and Jones. (Courtesy Kevin Skinner)

Another race, another DNF for Grant. His motor blew on lap 71 in the Kent race. (Courtesy Kevin Skinner)

Top left: The #4 Javelin was driven by Lew Florence at Pacific Raceways. He had a troubled race, finishing 15th, 24 laps down on the winner. (Courtesy Kevin Skinner)

Above: Hunter lasted until lap 32 (of 135) before his motor expired. (Courtesy Kevin Skinner)

Left: The Dave Tatum 1967 Mercury Cougar was bought by Bill Pendleton, who painted it yellow and raced it in 1969. Pendleton co-drove the car with Tatum during some of its earliest outings in 1967. He picked up $350 for finishing eighth here at Pacific Raceways. (Courtesy Kevin Skinner)

trophy for third. Jerry Grant completed just 12 laps before the motor cried enough, but team-mate Grable coaxed the other factory Javelin home in sixth, one position and two laps ahead of Ron Hunter. Ted Roberts was a retirement. David Hobbs was invited to drive the second T/G Racing Firebird at Riverside, but he too retired.

And so it was that neither of the factory AMC Javelins nor Pontiac Firebirds won a Trans-Am race in 1969. After the first few races, few would have bet against Ford reasserting itself at the top. But despite packing only half the firepower, Penske Racing brought Chevrolet its second Manufacturers' Championship in succession.

Chevrolet won the 1969 Trans-Am Manufacturers' Championship with 78 points to the 64 of Ford. Pontiac was third on 32, with American Motors on 13, some of which had been amassed by the independents.

And so while neither AMC nor Pontiac won a race, by the same token, neither manufacturer spent anywhere near as much as Ford, which reportedly pumped $3.8 million into its 1969 Trans-Am program. It could be suggested – on the criterion of money versus reward – that Ford was the biggest loser of the 1969 Trans-Am.

Although the little T/G Racing crew came up winless, Jerry Titus partnered with Jon Ward to run the T5.0 class at the 1969 Daytona 24 Hours. The pair shared the same Firebird Titus had driven in the Kent final in 1968. This was the car originally built by Ward from a 1967 Camaro, said to be his mother's street car! Although not a round of the Trans-Am Championship, the pairing not only won their class, but also finished third outright, beaten only by a pair of Lola T70 MkIIB sports prototypes. Indeed, it was the Penske Racing T70, driven by Mark Donohue and Chuck Parsons, which won the race.

Top right: Riverside Raceway hosted the final round of the 1969 Trans-Am, and the Kaplan Javelin team's season had been a tough one. This photo capturing Grant was snapped very early in the race, for he lasted just 12 laps before the engine popped. (Courtesy John Mensinger)

Right: Again, Jerry Titus produced a top-class result, finishing here at Riverside in third, behind the two Penske Racing Camaros. His little team didn't have the budget enjoyed by the other factory outfits, but they punched above their weight. (Courtesy John Mensinger)

1970

In the months that separated the final 1969 Trans-Am race in October, and the first 1970 race in April, the SCCA introduced wholesale changes that would ultimately result in more manufacturers entering the series, and produce closer racing.

For the first time since the inception of the Trans-Am, engine sizes larger than 5000cc in stock form could be reduced in size to meet the maximum limit. And as a result, the 1970 championship would feature factory teams from all the big four American manufacturers for the first time: General Motors, Ford Motor Company, American Motors Corporation, and finally, Chrysler Corporation.

Six different name plates would compete with full factory funding: Ford Mustang, Chevrolet Camaro, Pontiac Firebird, AMC Javelin, Dodge Challenger, and Plymouth Barracuda.

Other new freedoms included brakes. Teams could fit any brakes they wished to and there was no longer the messy procedure of offering production street cars with race brake package options that were very expensive and very few customers ordered.

And finally, a new rule was introduced regarding bodywork. Or, more specifically, front chin spoilers. Previously, Trans-Am bodywork requirements were strict. No surprises given they were based on FIA Group 2. Essentially, any external body part, be it a spoiler, vent or scoop, had to be an option on the street car. Most manufacturers produced a special Trans-Am homologation model fitted with a chin spoiler so it could be carried across to the race car. But for 1970, this was no longer a requirement. For 1970, front spoilers were free. However, the rules stated they had to be mounted to the front body underside, not extend beyond the front bumper, be no wider than the vehicle's front wheel track centerline, not extend more than 4in below the bodywork, and be as unobtrusive as possible when viewed from a side profile. So, not altogether free. In fact, a flat sheet of aluminum with some brake vent holes was basically what the SCCA was allowing.

However, every other external body component carried across to the race car had to be fitted to a variant of the street car. And so, essentially, manufacturers still needed to produce a homologation special. And that's exactly what they did. Ford had the Mustang Boss 302, Chevrolet the Camaro Z28, Pontiac the Firebird Trans-Am, AMC the Mark Donohue Special, and the new guys, Chrysler, unveiled the Dodge Challenger T/A and Plymouth 'Cuda All American Racers (AAR).

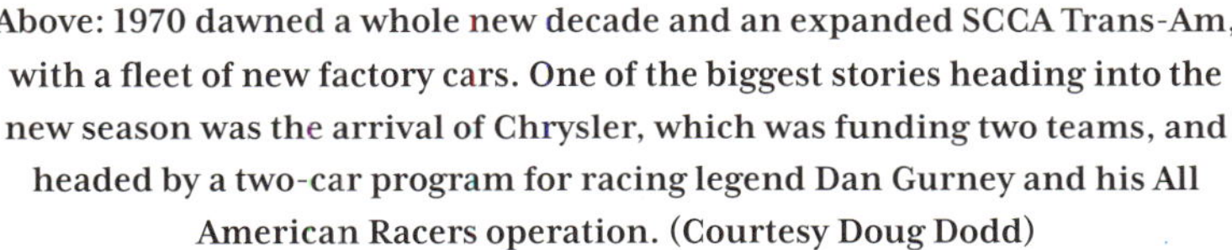
Above: 1970 dawned a whole new decade and an expanded SCCA Trans-Am, with a fleet of new factory cars. One of the biggest stories heading into the new season was the arrival of Chrysler, which was funding two teams, and headed by a two-car program for racing legend Dan Gurney and his All American Racers operation. (Courtesy Doug Dodd)

Top right: While Gurney himself would drive the #48 Plymouth Cuda, his young protégé Swede Savage would drive the 42 car. (Courtesy Doug Dodd)

Right: The second Chrysler team was the single-car operation run by Ray Caldwell at Autodynamics, who was partnered with Sam Posey. The Autodynamics Dodge Challenger was painted in an unmistakable Sublime Green, a factory hue applied at the instruction of Chrysler. Dodge produced a homologation special called the Challenger T/A, on which several special parts were carried across to the race car, including the outrageous hood scoop. The impressive green machine finished sixth at Laguna Seca. (Courtesy Doug Dodd)

But while the SCCA gave with one hand, it took with the other. For 1970, production requirements for homologation specials increased to a minimum 2500 units, or 1/250th of the preceding year's total production, whichever was greater. These units had to be built by 15 May, with the paperwork filed by 1 June.

In previous years, the SCCA allowed multiple carburetors; two four-barrels or four two-barrels. For 1970, however, only a single four-barrel was allowed, no matter what the street cars had.

Also, the 1970 minimum weight limit for O2 Trans-Am cars increased to 3200 pounds dry, or 3400 pounds ready to race.

As it had done in 1969, the SCCA scheduled 12 rounds for the 1970 Trans-Am Championship, for which there was still no drivers' championship,

despite the international star quality of its pilots. Go figure. The championship kicked off at Laguna Seca on 19 April, followed by a new race in Dallas, Texas, at a brand-new facility in Lewisville. There followed Lime Rock, Bryar, Mid-Ohio, Bridgehampton, Donnybrooke, Road America, Circuit Mont-Tremblant, Watkins Glen, Seattle, and it concluded at Riverside on 4 October.

For the first time since its inception, the Trans-Am was split into separate races for the U2 and O2 classes. Both classes were held the same weekend at the same track, but the U2 races were contested on the Saturday, with the O2 cars on Sunday as the main event.

Beyond the various SCCA regulation tweaks, there was a lot of action happening behind closed doors between the teams and manufacturers. The

Clockwise from far left: The AAR operation was truly impressive, and crowds gathered in the Laguna Seca pits to get a closer look. New-for-1970 regulations allowed non-factory front spoilers, and the neat items on the Cudas included ducting holes for the front brakes. AAR built its own motors with parts developed and supplied by Keith Black. Here at Laguna Seca, Gurney lasted until lap 21 of 90 when the gearbox broke, while Savage went on to finish fourth. (Courtesy Doug Dodd)

The AAR Cudas were finished in an attractive metallic blue, as per all AAR cars of the era. That was the power that Gurney packed. Chrysler didn't dictate the color scheme. Toy company Mattel came on board as a sponsor with its Hot Wheels brand. The Plymouth Trans-Am homologation special was called the AAR Cuda, and, like the T/A Challenger, sported a collection of performance parts, including its own unique hood with central hump and Naca duct. The red and orange stripes on the rear valance would be replicated on the hood within a couple of races. (Courtesy Doug Dodd)

This was an interesting entry at Laguna Seca. Todco traveled all the way from Canada with this 1969 Pontiac Firebird for Craig Fisher. This was a T/G Racing built car, but note it has the correct nose, and not that which the T/G cars were forced to run in 1969. It was Pontiac powered, which of course was its downfall. Fisher lasted until lap 60 when, inevitably, the motor broke. (Courtesy Doug Dodd)

The colorful, raucous Trans-Am field rolls down the Laguna Seca hill ready to begin the first race of the season. After 90 laps of hard racing, the end result had a familiar look to it. Bud Moore Mustangs finished first and third, while Mark Donohue was second. Of course, Penske Racing was now the factory AMC squad. (Courtesy Doug Dodd)

biggest news was that Penske Racing had parted ways with Chevrolet and signed a new multi-million dollar, multi-year contract with American Motors to build and campaign the factory Javelins. It was a major coup for both parties.

Sports car racing legend and oil tycoon Jim Hall, of Chapparal Cars fame, would take over the Camaro program. Hall already enjoyed a close relationship with General Motors.

After its two-pronged attack on the 1969 Trans-Am that ultimately ended in defeat, Ford downsized its efforts by funding just one team. Shelby was dropped, with Bud Moore Engineering going it alone, campaigning two Boss 302 Mustangs for Farnelli Jones and George Follmer.

The little T/G Racing team went from one extreme to the other. Having built half a dozen cars in 1969 for themselves and a handful of independents, T/G switched to a single-car team in 1970, with Pontiac's new second-generation Firebird.

And finally, Dan Gurney's AAR and the partnership of driver Sam Posey and Ray Caldwell of Autodynamics would run the exciting new Plymouth and Dodge pony car entries.

Chrysler Corporation

In late 1969, Chrysler introduced its curvy cousins, the E-Body Dodge Challenger and Plymouth Barracuda. This pair of Mopar beauties were offered with a wide range of engine choices, from the rugged base-model 225in^3 in-line six, 318, 340 and 383in^3 small-block V8s, the 440in^3 big-block V8, and the Hemi-headed 426in^3 big-block V8. And under the old Trans-Am engine rules, none would have been suitable, but with the regulation change, Chrysler finally made its long-awaited arrival, not including its lukewarm 1966 effort.

The first-generation Plymouth Barracuda and third-generation Dodge Dart were targeted at the same youth market as the Ford Mustang when it arrived in 1964. But both widely missed the mark. These were essentially two-door variants of Chrysler's multipurpose platform volume sellers, available in a wide range of body styles to appease varied buyer requirements. This included a station wagon and a four-door. If there was one thing the Mustang did extremely well, it was to disassociate itself from Ford's more mundane subjects, even if its underpinning was adopted from the lowly Falcon.

Although the second-generation Barracuda, launched for the 1967 model year, was a far more convincing effort, it was still a Valiant; it was still a sporty makeover of the station wagon moms drove to get the groceries. So too the fourth-gen Dart.

But in late 1969, Chrysler launched its E-Body siblings: the Dodge Challenger and Plymouth Barracuda. Finally, Chrysler did what it should have done years earlier, and what Mercury, Chevrolet, Pontiac, and even little ole' American Motors were already doing – create a standalone pony car to rival the Mustang.

To retain the status quo, Chrysler continued the Dart, unaffected by the arrival of its E-Body models, and introduced the Plymouth Duster, which shared the low-buck Valiant platform and nose, but had a unique two-door body. Both the Dart and Duster shared lower base prices and more basic equipment than the new E-Body pony cars.

At first glance the Barracuda and Challenger appeared almost one

Top: Bryar hosted Round three of the 1970 Trans-Am, and Savage qualified second fastest to Jones. But wait, where is Gurney? Following the opening event at Laguna Seca, Chrysler informed the team it was slashing its racing budget, and as such, AAR soldiered on as a single-car operation. Savage was thus moved into Gurney's #48 Cuda. His engine broke at one-third distance. On the second row is Donohue's Penske Javelin, which finished third, three laps down on winner Jones, and one place back from his new team-mate Peter Revson. (Courtesy Autosportsltd.com)

Above: On the fourth row of the Bryar grid was Jerry Titus in the new-for-1970 T/G Racing Pontiac Firebird. The slick-looking second-generation Firebird was finally using Pontiac power, which would be its Achilles heel, being heavy, underpowered, and unreliable. Titus was a spectator after just five laps, which was three laps more than Craig Fisher's Pontiac-powered 1969 Firebird could muster. (Courtesy Autosportsltd.com)

The Penske team rolls Donohue's Javelin out of the transporter at Mid-Ohio for Round four of the 1970 Trans-Am. Naturally, Penske invested heavily in making its cars as neat and attractive as they could be, with countless beautiful details, including the front spoiler, and even the pin striping on the hood. (Courtesy Raynald Bélanger Collection)

And here comes Revson's Penske Javelin. One of the 'unfair advantages' of the Penske team in 1970 was to use four-lug wheels, which required special Minilites be created. Trans-Am cars all performed so evenly that any small advantage needed to be explored, and Penske rightly figured that it only took 80 percent of the time to swap wheels with four lugs during a pit stop as it did those with five lugs. (Courtesy Raynald Bélanger Collection)

and the same, but there were subtle differences. Firstly, in keeping with Chrysler's tiered nameplate system, the Challenger came with a 110in wheelbase, 2in longer than that of the Barracuda. While both employed the popular 'Coke bottle' side profile, the Challenger sported slightly softer lines, including the top rear corner of the side windows, while the Barracuda featured a more abrupt directional change. Both models had a horizontal sculpture line running down the flanks. On the Barracuda it was perfectly straight, while on the Challenger it curved up and over the rear wheel openings, following the lines of the rear quarters. The Challenger had a more rounded rump than the Barracuda, and, naturally, carried four headlights to the two of the Barracuda. All subtle differences, but all designed to impress upon buyers that the Dodge was higher up on the Chrysler food chain. But, still, the pair were very clearly related.

The Chrysler E-Body models were broad by pony car standards, at 76.1in wide. By comparison, a 1970 Mustang was 71.7in, and a new second-generation Camaro was 74.4in.

Chrysler offered two body styles on the Challenger and Barracuda: the two-door hardtop and a convertible.

Two factory Chrysler teams would be funded in the 1970 Trans-Am, ensuring both its E-Body entries were represented. Dan Gurney's AAR fielded a pair of Plymouths, while the pairing of Ray Caldwell and Sam Posey ran a single Dodge.

Plymouth Cuda

Dan Gurney was already a true American racing hero by 1970. He'd done it all, from winning a Formula 1 race in his own car, to competing at the very

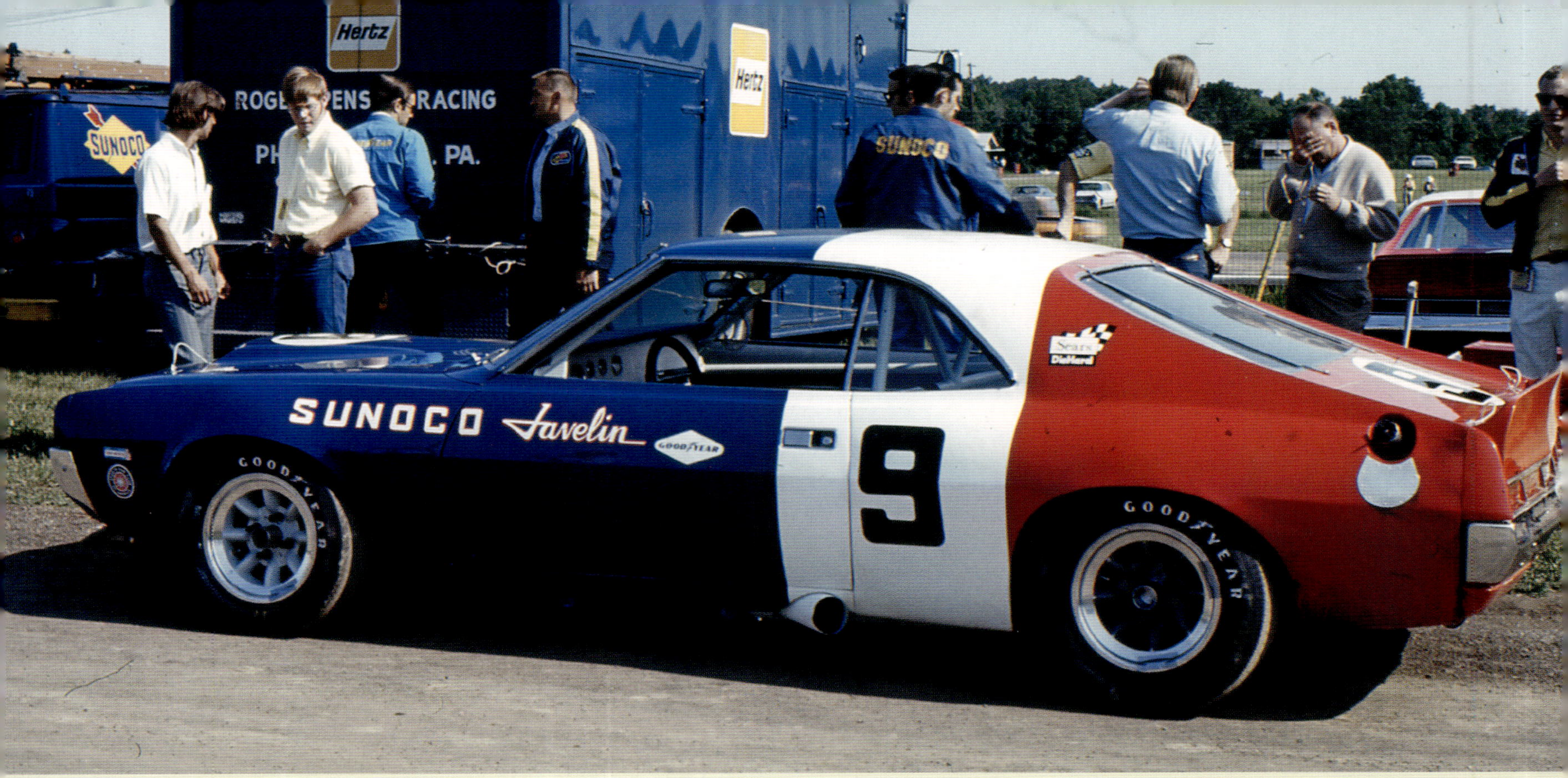
Hertz
SUNOCO
RACING
PA.
SUNOCO Javelin
GOOD YEAR
9
Sears DieHard

SUNOCO Javelin

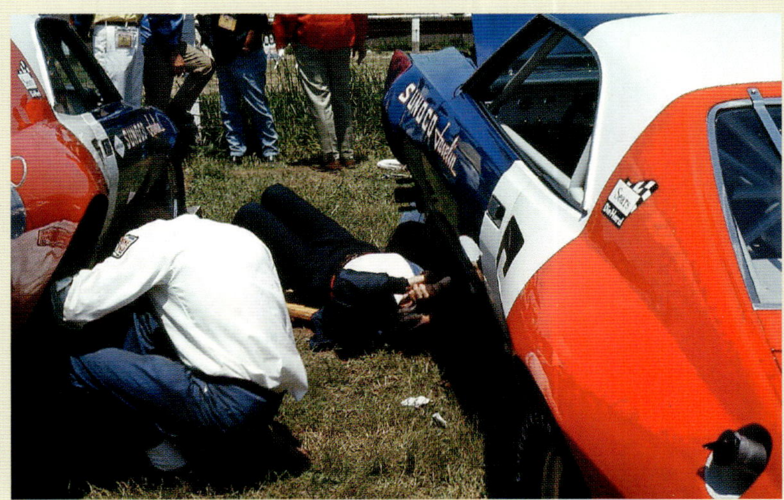

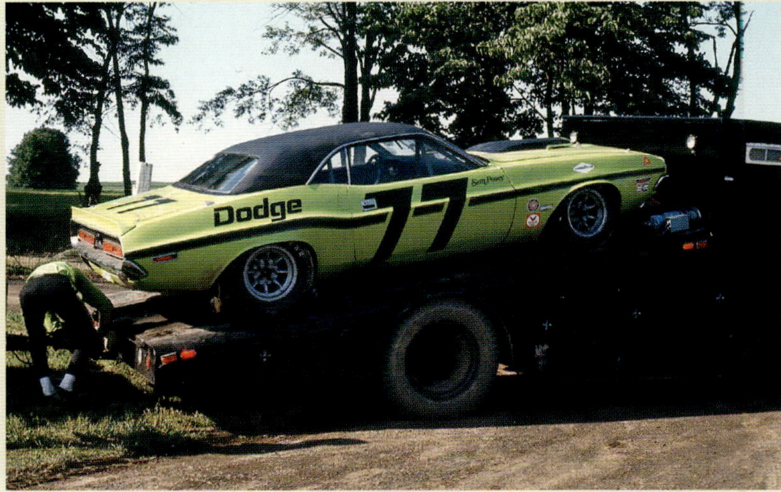

Dodge
77

Opposite top: Revson's immaculate Penske Javelin rests in the Mid-Ohio pits. Note the neat exhaust system tucked up into the rockers to provide extra ground clearance. The Penske crew even crafted an aluminum plate beneath the fuel filler to protect the paint. New-for-1970 Trans-Am rules required cars be fueled with a hand-held dump can, and have a screw-in fuel cap, all to avoid the crazy fuel towers that caused so much drama in 1969. (Courtesy Raynald Bélanger Collection)

Bottom left: From this angle can be seen the subtle but beautifully crafted fender flares on the two factory Javelins. (Courtesy Raynald Bélanger Collection)

Bottom right: The Autodynamics team arrives at Mid-Ohio with its Dodge Challenger. Sam Posey hated the green paint, so covered up as much of it as he could with matt black, including the roof. The body on this car wasn't properly neutralized after it was acid-dipped, and the team was constantly having to weld up cracks where it broke apart from the stresses of racing. The matt black paint on the roof was a good way to disguise stress cracks. (Courtesy Raynald Bélanger Collection)

Top right: The AAR crew carries out pre-race preparation on Savage's Cuda alongside the team's impressive transporter. The guy in the American Motors jacket sizes up the competition. Both the Cudas and Challengers sat very low to the ground. From this angle can be seen part of the complex roll cage structure on the passenger side designed with computers. (Courtesy Raynald Bélanger Collection)

Right: T/G Racing arrives at Mid-Ohio with its Firebird. Compare this team's mode of transport with that of AAR. Following its hectic 1969 Trans-Am program where it built and raced two cars and then built several more to be sold and leased to independent teams, T/G Racing ran just a single-car program in 1970. (Courtesy Raynald Bélanger Collection)

The T/G Firebird sported an assortment of different exhaust layouts throughout the first half of 1970, including side pipes that exited halfway between the front and rear wheels and traveled along the side bodywork before dumping in front of the rear wheels, and this system, with two pipes exiting out the back. The troublesome Pontiac lump struggled for power, and trialing different exhaust designs was a good way to coax a little extra from it. Compare the brutal Firebird fender flares with those of the Penske Javelins. Of course, the street Firebird Trans-Am was appropriately brash, so this look was quite fitting. The single wide stripe running down the center replicated that of the street variant. The Autodynamics ramp truck can be seen in the background. (Courtesy Raynald Bélanger Collection)

For its second-generation Firebird, Pontiac produced the wild Trans-Am model, with a slew of homologation parts that could be carried across to the race cars. These included the special reverse-facing intake scoop attached to the motor that sucked in cool air via a hole in the hood. There was also a large three-piece rear spoiler, which Chevrolet would have to adopt on its second-generation Camaro. The 'wheel opening air spoilers', as Pontiac called them, which framed the wheel openings, likely helped air pass around the wheels more cleanly, while the air extractors in the front fenders helped hot air escape the engine bay. The SCCA required all cars race without door glass, so the door windows seen here would have only been used during transportation on the open hauler. (Courtesy Raynald Bélanger Collection)

highest levels in Indycar, Can-Am and the NASCAR Grand National. Gurney had dabbled in the Trans-Am when his other commitments allowed, and always with Ford products. Indeed, he'd enjoyed a long and prosperous career with Ford. But in 1970 he jumped ship.

Gurney announced in October 1969 that AAR and Chrysler were joining forces to run a pair of Plymouths in the 1970 Trans-Am. But the project started late, with the donor cars only arriving in early January, and the motors appearing later still. Chrysler funded AAR to the tune of $1 million.

Chrysler backed its two teams, and its Trans-Am effort as a whole, by producing a pair of homologation specials for both its new E-Body models. The Plymouth example was called the AAR Cuda (note, Plymouth marketed its high-performance Barracuda option as the abbreviated 'Cuda). The AAR Cuda was a street car featuring, among other components, a fiberglass hood with large central Naca duct, and rear-deck spoiler similar to that of the first-generation Camaro. Both the hood and spoiler were finished in satin black. A pair of small spoilers mounted on the front corners of the street version were added, but weren't actually required under the new-for-1970 front spoiler rule, and wouldn't have done anything useful anyway. As per Trans-Am rules, all the bodywork upgrades could be carried across to the race cars.

AAR employed some pretty smart operators, including the legendary Phil Remington, who'd previously worked for Lance Reventlow (heir to the Woolworth fortune) on the Scarab sports and F1 cars, and Shelby American. Also joining the program was engineer and designer Bob Tarozzi.

Between AAR and Autodynamics, AAR was the bigger operation, and as such, all the chassis design and fabrication work for both models would be carried out by AAR. Tarozzi oversaw the complex roll cage layout and construction, formulated partly with computers.

Before any fabrication work began on the Cuda and Challenger race cars, the bare bodies were sent off to be acid-dipped, which was a process all the factory teams were now employing. Even at the new-for-1970 minimum weight limit, the Chrysler teams had some trouble getting their cars down to the weight of their rivals. In stock form, the Chryslers weighed 3585 pounds, compared with the 3122 pounds of the Mustang Boss 302 and 3313 of the Camaro Z28. So they were pretty hefty from the outset.

Following the dipping process, the bodies were returned to AAR and bolted to a chassis plate, designed and built by Tarozzi. And from there, the fabrication work started.

The Chryslers employed torsion bar front suspension as standard, and Tarozzi focused on getting the cars to sit as low to the ground as the rules would allow. In fact, the front sway bar had to be routed through the oil pan. The rear suspension layout on the AAR cars featured double adjustable Koni shock absorbers mounted either side of the axle to help reduce axle tramp, and horizontal shocks for the same purpose, plus a Panhard bar.

Keith Black, best known for his winning drag racing and stock car motors, carried out engine development work for the Chrysler Trans-Am program, although AAR largely built its own engines using parts supplied by Black. Because Chrysler didn't have a motor that fit within the 5000cc Trans-Am limit, the 340 was de-stroked. Both the Cudas and Challengers used Chrysler A833-based four-speed transmission from the NASCAR program, and there was supposedly at least one transmission casing cast from aluminum, to save weight, but with metal shavings in the paint to pass the SCCA magnet test. The Plymouth and Dodge Trans-Am cars were fitted with a rear end sporting an aluminum diff head.

The Cudas rolled on eight-spoke Minilite wheels and Goodyear tires, while brakes were Kelsey-Hayes.

AAR planned to field two Cudas throughout the 1970 Trans-Am, to be driven by Gurney and his rapid young protégé, David 'Swede' Savage. The two Cudas were painted in the dark metallic blue of AAR, and sported the fiberglass hood and rear-deck spoiler from the AAR street car. The Minilites had the centers painted white. Beautiful details abounded, including the neat chin spoiler with brake cooling ducts, and a fiberglass duct attached to the driver's side A-pillar to deliver cool air. Most teams simply used flexible pipe and race tape for this task.

Huge, bold white numbers were carried on the doors: number 48 for Gurney, and 42 for Savage. White Plymouth lettering adorned the front fenders, with a number on the hood above the Naca duct. In early promotional material, the AAR Cudas wore the broken side stripes of the street cars, but these had disappeared by the first round of the championship. However, AAR Cuda decals, as per the street-going Cuda, were a feature of the rear quarters. From Round four at Mid-Ohio, bright red, orange and yellow stripes followed the diagonal shape of the Naca duct on the hood. AAR picked up sponsorship from Mattel with his Hot Wheels brand.

In all, AAR built three Cudas for its 1970 Trans-Am program, and a further two Challenger shells which were dispatched to Autodynamics after acid-dipping, roll cage structure, and basic fabrication work was complete.

Following Round three of the championship at Lime Rock, Chrysler informed Gurney that it was slashing its race program funding and, with that, AAR entered just one Cuda for Savage from Round four. However, Gurney made a comeback in the final two races at Seattle and Riverside, but financed the addition of the second car himself.

Dodge Challenger

Sam Posey and Ray Caldwell first teamed up in 1963 when Caldwell's Autodynamics shop was producing Formula Vees. Posey had family money and, after a successful Formula Ford partnership, financed a Group 7 Can-Am car called the Caldwell D7, which was, naturally, designed, built and campaigned by Ray Caldwell.

Posey was a naturally talented driver, but had the financial means to fund his racing, and that's exactly what he did. In 1968, he bought himself a seat in the second Penske Camaro for four Trans-Am events, and paid Roger Penske $4000 per race for the privilege. No race wins were forthcoming. However, he placed second in one race, and third in the other three. And then, in a one-off appearance for Shelby in 1969 at Lime Rock, he won!

Posey's race results no doubt helped when Caldwell decided he wanted to snag a factory Trans-Am deal for 1970. There was Caldwell's slick presentation, too. Also, Peter Hutchinson was in charge of Chrysler's racing programs. Hutchinson was a former editor for *Car and Driver* magazine and,

Left: The small rear deck spoiler was shared on both the Challenger and Cuda, and appeared on the street-going T/A Challenger and AAR Cuda specifically to be homologated for the Trans-Am. The Autodynamics Challenger had its basic fabrication, including roll cage, built by AAR. (Courtesy Raynald Bélanger Collection)

Below: Mid-Ohio hosted Round four of the 1970 Trans-Am Championship, and while an increasingly desperate Penske Racing put up a good fight, ultimately, Ford won again. Donohue battled Follmer's Bud Moore Mustang for a time, but the Mustang driver was in front when it mattered, trailing his team-mate home. Donohue finished a frustrated third, but at least he was on the same lap as the dominant Fords. (Courtesy Autosportsltd.com)

Top left: Pace lap for the 1970 Road America Trans-Am race at Elkhart Lake. The Fords were devastating in qualifying, but all hell broke loose in the first turn when Ed Leslie, seen here on the second row alongside Savage, squeezed between them. Posey spent a chunk of the race leading in his Dodge, until Donohue popped up late in the race after a brilliant Penske strategy to pit out of sync to avoid the traffic and pit lane carnage, and took the first Javelin Trans-Am win. (Courtesy Larry Fulhorst)

Above: Dan Spiegel contested the Road America Trans-Am in his charismatic 1966 Chevy Nova. From a field of 37 entries, the biggest yet, Spiegel finished 23rd. (Courtesy Peter Luongo Photo)

Left: The impressive AAR camp setup at Circuit Mont-Tremblant, Round eight of the 1970 Trans-Am. (Courtesy Autosportsltd.com)

Above: Inside the Ted Roberts AMC Javelin. This was one of Ron Kaplan's factory cars from 1969, which he updated for Roberts, who ran most of the 1970 schedule, including here at Circuit Mont-Tremblant. (Courtesy Autosportsltd.com)

Top left: After racing a 1969 Firebird in the early 1970 races, the Todco team built this second-generation Firebird which made its Trans-Am debut at Circuit Mont-Tremblant. It was driven by Derek Johnson. (Courtesy Yves St-Jean)

Above: Derek Johnson's office inside the Todco Firebird. By 1970 it was rare for a Trans-Am sedan not to have a driver headrest. Compare the basic roll cage of this car with some of the elaborate cages of the latest factory cars. (Courtesy Yves St-Jean)

Top right: The Pontiac mill powering the new Todco Firebird. Although this car featured the homologated rear-facing air intake, it was molded into the hood, rather than mounted on the motor. (Courtesy Yves St-Jean)

Above: Mark Donohue gets comfortable inside his Penske Javelin. (Courtesy Yves St-Jean)

Left, top to bottom: The brilliant Swede Savage. By the Circuit Mont-Tremblant race, he'd already put his AAR Cuda on pole more than once, but a race win still eluded him. (Courtesy Yves St-Jean)

This superb photo shows the intricacies of the roll cage structure in the AAR Cuda, with bars filling the passenger compartment, then linking both sides of the transmission tunnel. The matting on the floor reduced engine and transmission heat, while the molded driver's air vent wrapped neatly around the A-pillar. (Courtesy Yves St-Jean)

The beautiful workmanship of the AAR engine bay. AAR built its own motors, whereas the Autodynamics team's was built by Keith Black. It's believed the Keith Black motors made a little more power. (Courtesy Yves St-Jean)

Opposite top: For the Trans-Am race at Circuit Mont-Tremblant, 37 cars started. Jones was on pole, with Donohue starting next to him. (Courtesy Autosportsltd.com)

Opposite bottom: Moments after the race start, and with the leaders having just gone through, Savage, Posey and Revson all fight to establish their positions. (Courtesy Autosportsltd.com)

in 1967, wrote a story on the Caldwell D7. From there a relationship was established, which no doubt helped cement the Autodynamics Chrysler Trans-Am deal. Many assumed former Chrysler Trans-Am racer Bob Tullius would get the gig, but this came to nothing.

With AAR based in California, and Autodynamics in Marblehead, Massachusetts, the operation was relocated to Long Beach to work more closely with AAR. Among those on the Autodynamics payroll were Carroll Smith, who'd overseen Fords Le Mans GT40 program, and fabricator Jack McCormack, who'd later manufacturer his own Formula 5000 cars.

Like the AAR Cuda, Dodge produced a homologation special version of the Challenger, called the Challenger T/A (Trans-Am). It was similar to the AAR Cuda under the surface, and shared the same rear-deck spoiler. The Challenger also featured a fiberglass hood with a scoop, although this was a lurid, raised snorkel device with twin openings. The Challenger T/A sported a pair of small chin spoilers but, again, these would not be carried across to the race cars. Like the AAR Cuda, the hood and deck spoiler were painted satin black, as were the chin spoilers.

The Challenger T/A carried a bold graphics package with a wide stripe

Mileage
Player's
Shell

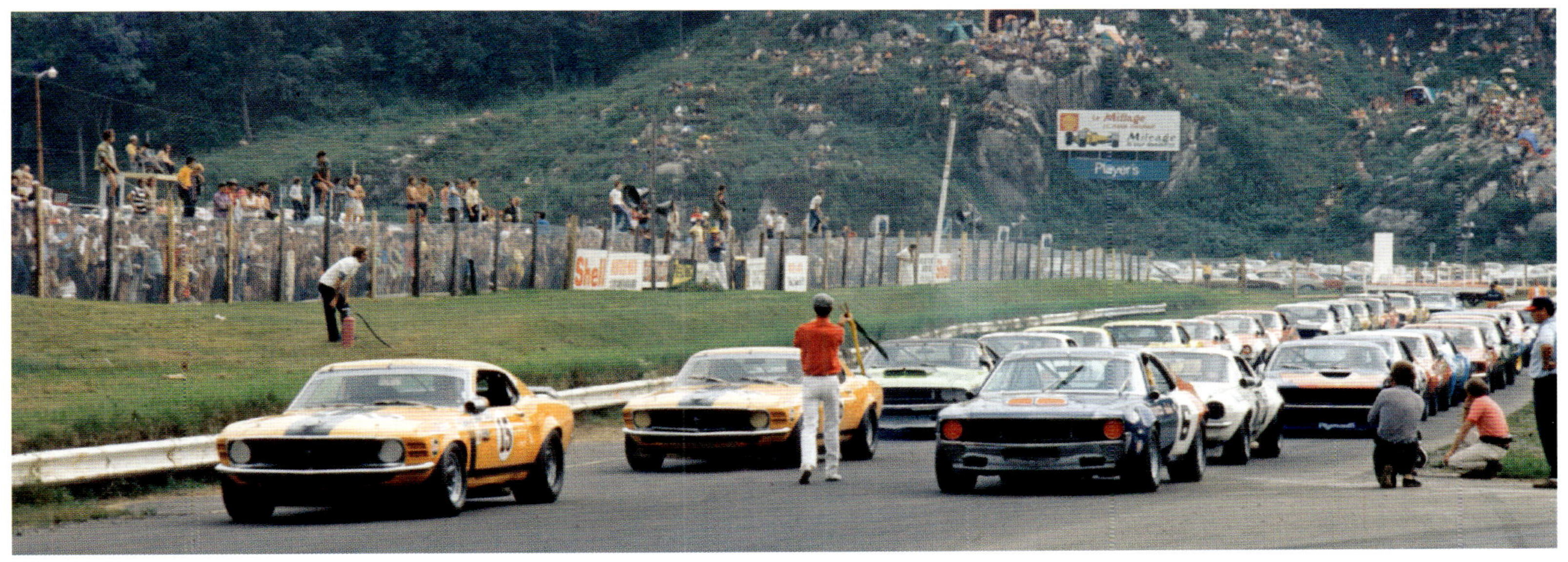

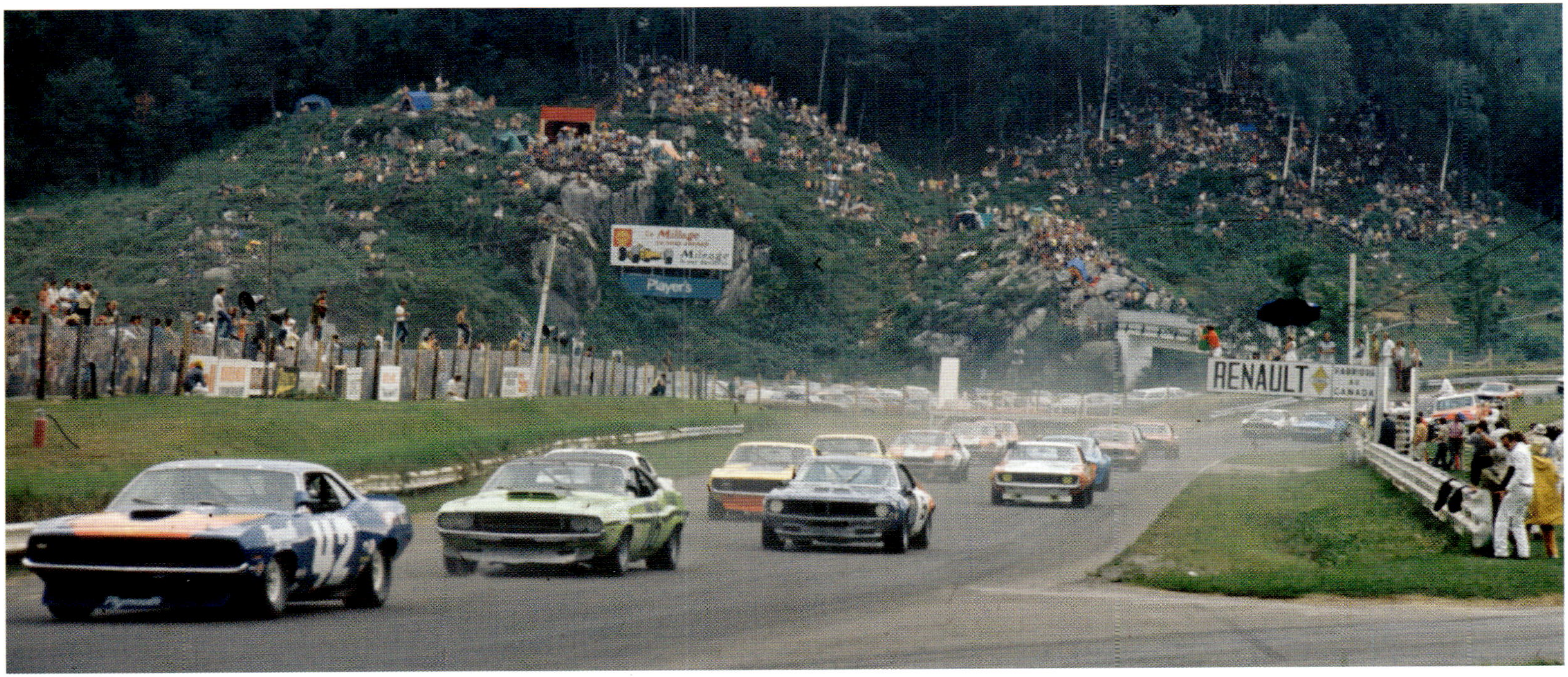
Mileage
Player's
RENAULT

Left: Michael Tremblay held the honor of being the first retirement at Circuit Mont-Tremblant. His elderly Mercury Cougar lasted just one lap. (Courtesy Denis Giguère)

Below: Posey battles his way through some of the lapped cars in his effort to stay ahead of the Chaparral Camaro. Bob Biernerth is in the 1969 Camaro, while at the rear of this gaggle is the Mustang of Steve Ross. (Courtesy Denis Giguère)

running from the nose and ending abruptly in line with the rear of the side glass, broken on the front fenders with T/A lettering.

AAR supplied two Challenger bodies to Autodynamics, with the roll cages and other fabrication completed. Of course, the bodies had been acid-dipped prior to beginning fabrication work. The dipping process allows the acid to eat at the metal, lightening it, before being neutralized. The Challenger bodies, however, weren't neutralized correctly and the acid kept doing its work. This would prove an ongoing bugbear for Autodynamics throughout the season, and the team was constantly having to weld cracks between races and add bracing.

The Autodynamics Challenger race cars were more or less the same as the AAR Cudas, but whereas AAR built its engines in-house, using development parts supplied by Keith Black, Autodynamics ordered what were essentially Keith Black crate motors, ready to be dropped straight into the race car. The Black-built motors were considered some of the best in the Trans-Am paddock in 1970.

Where the Autodynamics Challengers differed from the AAR Cudas was in the rear suspension design. Coming from an open-wheeler and sports car background, Caldwell attempted to apply some of these principles into the Challenger with his own Watts-link design.

Opposite top left: Derek Johnson's race at Circuit Mont-Tremblant was painfully short. The Pontiac motor broke on lap three. (Courtesy Autosportsltd.com)

Opposite, far right: The two Penske Javelins running line astern. Revson looks to have done a little panel rubbing with another car. (Courtesy Autosportsltd.com)

Opposite: Ted Roberts leads one of the ARA Camaros. (Courtesy Autosportsltd.com)

Interestingly, while Gurney could paint his Cudas any color he pleased, Chrysler's directive to Autodynamics was that its Challengers be finished in sublime green, a Chrysler factory hue that Posey hated! He attempted to numb the green intensity by painting the roof black. Huge black racing numbers adorned the doors.

Like the Cudas, the Autodynamics Challengers rolled on Minilite wheels.

Unlike AAR, Autodynamics contested the 1970 Trans-Am Championship as a one-car team, with Posey doing the driving. For this program, Posey was a paid driver. As the season neared its end, and with Chrysler clearly going cold on its Trans-Am participation, Autodynamics completed construction of its second Challenger, which was driven by Ron Bucknum in Seattle, and Tony Adamowicz at Riverside.

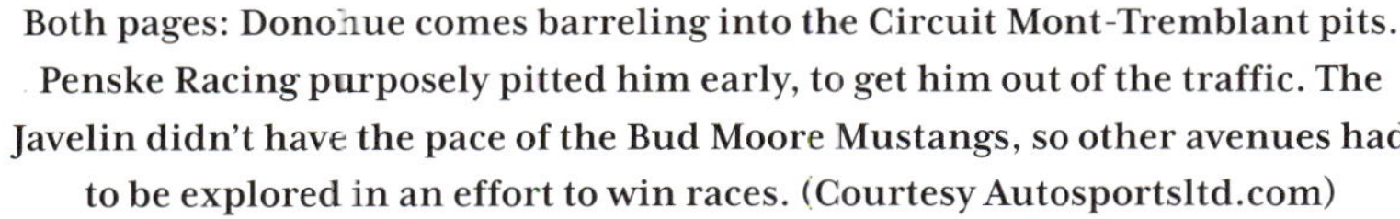

Both pages: Donohue comes barreling into the Circuit Mont-Tremblant pits. Penske Racing purposely pitted him early, to get him out of the traffic. The Javelin didn't have the pace of the Bud Moore Mustangs, so other avenues had to be explored in an effort to win races. (Courtesy Autosportsltd.com)

AMC Javelin

Penske Racing

Roger Penske had a close working relationship with General Motors and Chevrolet. Indeed, he was a Chevrolet dealer, and for what it was worth, given that no money was involved, apparently, Penske Racing was the Camaro Trans-Am factory team from when the model first debuted in early 1967. It was an engineering relationship, and it worked well. Penske generated income for the Trans-Am program through sponsorship, such as Sunoco Oil.

And so, in a fairly brave move, Penske Racing signed a three-year deal to run the AMC racing programs from 1970, to the tune of $2 million, which were spearheaded by the Javelin Trans-Am cars but would later diversify into the NASCAR Grand National stock car racing with the full-sized Matadore, and even Formula 5000.

On leaving Chevrolet, Penske Racing took Don Cox with them. Cox was a Chevrolet engineer who'd played a pivotal role in the Penske/Camaro Trans-Am success.

AMC treated the Javelin to a redesigned nose for 1970. An interesting new engine option was a 304in^3 motor, which for the first time fit the Trans-Am maximum size perfectly. But then, for 1970, the SCCA allowed de-stroking, so it was largely for nothing, as Traco Engineering used the 360 unit as the basis for the Penske Trans-Am race motors.

For its 1970 Trans-Am challenger, American Motors produced the 'Mark

The Autodynamics team services Posey's Challenger. (Courtesy Autosportsltd.com)

Donohue Special', which was an SST with extra bits to be carried over to the race cars. These included a Don Cox-designed rear-deck spoiler, which was a first-generation Camaro spoiler adapted to fit the Javelin. There was also a special hood with a large bulge in the middle. This was actually the 1970 AMX hood with the two faux vents at the front of the bulge made functional, to produce a ram-air system. The Javelin also featured a front chin spoiler that, like every other 1970 Homologation Special from Ford, Chevrolet, Pontiac, Dodge and Plymouth, wouldn't actually appear on the race cars because of the new front spoiler rule.

Penske Racing, headed by the brilliant driver and engineer Mark Donohue, didn't use any of the Ron Kaplan cars that American Motors passed over as part of the arrangement. Instead, they built two new cars from scratch, using brand-new 1970 Javelins.

Because the Penske deal went public shortly after the final round of the 1969 Trans-Am, some of the team stayed on after the Riverside event to test one of the Kaplan cars, and to get a feel for what they were working with.

Donohue wanted to run a 'gronked' rear axle arrangement to provide negative camber into the rear end. A lot of time was spent on this concept, with Don Cox creating an elaborate system by adding Oldsmobile Toronado front-wheel drive joints to the ends of the axles, hidden inside the housing. But after a lot of trouble, and much testing, the gronked axles really made no difference, so the concept was scrapped.

Penske Racing didn't try to reinvent the wheel. They made everything in the front suspension and upright area stronger, and AMC supplied uprights made from 4130 forged steel to which the spindles attached, positioned higher on the upright to lower the front of the car while still providing good suspension travel.

Cox designed the rear end with floating hubs and Watts-link, and also designed his own brake system, using Girling calipers. He introduced power assist on the front brakes to achieve 66/33 distribution front to rear. An initiative on the Penske Javelins was the use of special four-stud hubs, which also required special Minilite wheels to be cast with four stud holes instead of the regular five. The Penske Racing school of thought was that it took 80 percent of the time to undo and redo four studs as it did on five, saving time during pit stops.

The Penske Racing Javelins were one of the best handling Trans-Am cars in 1970, but the AMC motors were the weak link. Penske had Traco build the motors, which were down on power compared with the competition (except Pontiac) at around 375hp at the start of the year. Throughout the season, Traco managed to squeeze more from the AMC units, but they were never as good as those in the Mustangs.

Because the cornering speeds of the top Trans-Am cars were now so high, and because the SCCA still didn't allow dry-sump systems, the AMC motors suffered from oil starvation, and would break with no warning. The team made several sumps with baffles and trapdoors to try to control oil movement. They built the Javelins with removable front cross-members so they could switch out oil pans more easily. Following the season-opening race, the team ran a test day at Bryar, and Donohue had one of the crew sit in the back of the car, watching the oil pressure gauge while he lapped the track, and tap him on the shoulder every time the gauge dropped to zero. It dropped several times a lap!

The Penske Javelins had the motors positioned very low in the chassis to help lower the center of gravity. This contributed to the fluctuating oil pressure because the sumps were shallower. In the end, the team discovered the Bud Moore Mustangs were fitted with a secondary oil pump. Although dry-sump systems weren't allowed, oil pumps were free. So Penske Racing replaced its single-rotor pump with a pair of stacked rotors, each with a separate pickup. With that, the pickup from the second pump scavenged oil from the uphill section of the pan and filled the sump for the primary pump. This little trick solved the oil pressure problems.

Again, Penske Racing would run two cars, for Donohue and new signing Peter Revson. The team entered one car at the 1970 Daytona 24 Hours event, as a test bed for the upcoming Trans-Am season, but the motor failed after 205 laps due to oil starvation.

Because Donohue was so integral to the team, the Javelins were both built to his driving style. They had power brakes, but no power steering. But that's the way Donohue liked to drive them. And he was strong!

When Roger Penske publicly announced the new deal with American Motors to the press in late 1969, he said the team would win seven Trans-Am races in 1970. Even Donohue was surprised! In the end there were three wins, which was pretty impressive given the time frame Penske Racing had, the equipment it was working with, and the lack of proper engineering support from American Motors. But invariably, those wins came as a result of the team outsmarting the competition, and doing things differently, rather than enjoying all-out better speed, which it didn't have.

But the 1970 Penske Racing/American Motors Corporation Trans-Am program truly underlined just how good the Penske operation was. In many ways, it was a make-or-break season. It didn't win the Trans-Am Manufacturers' Championship, but it made a statement.

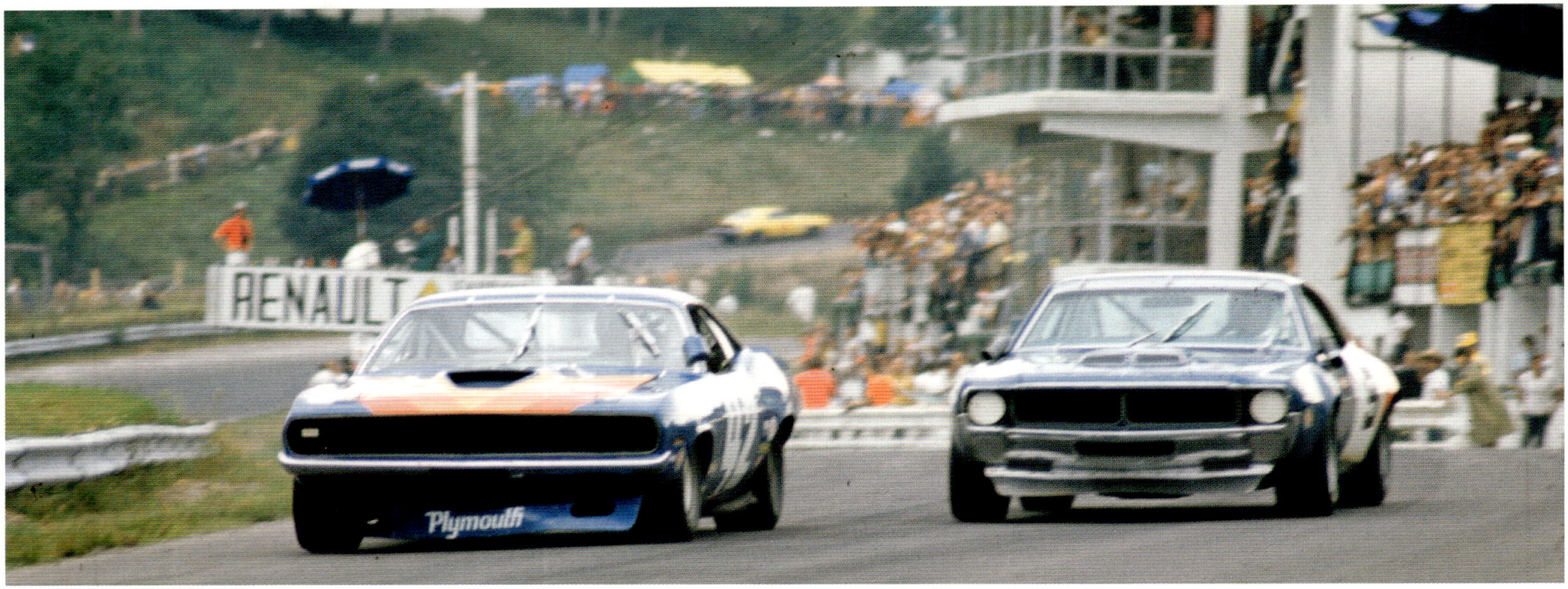
RENAULT
Plymouth

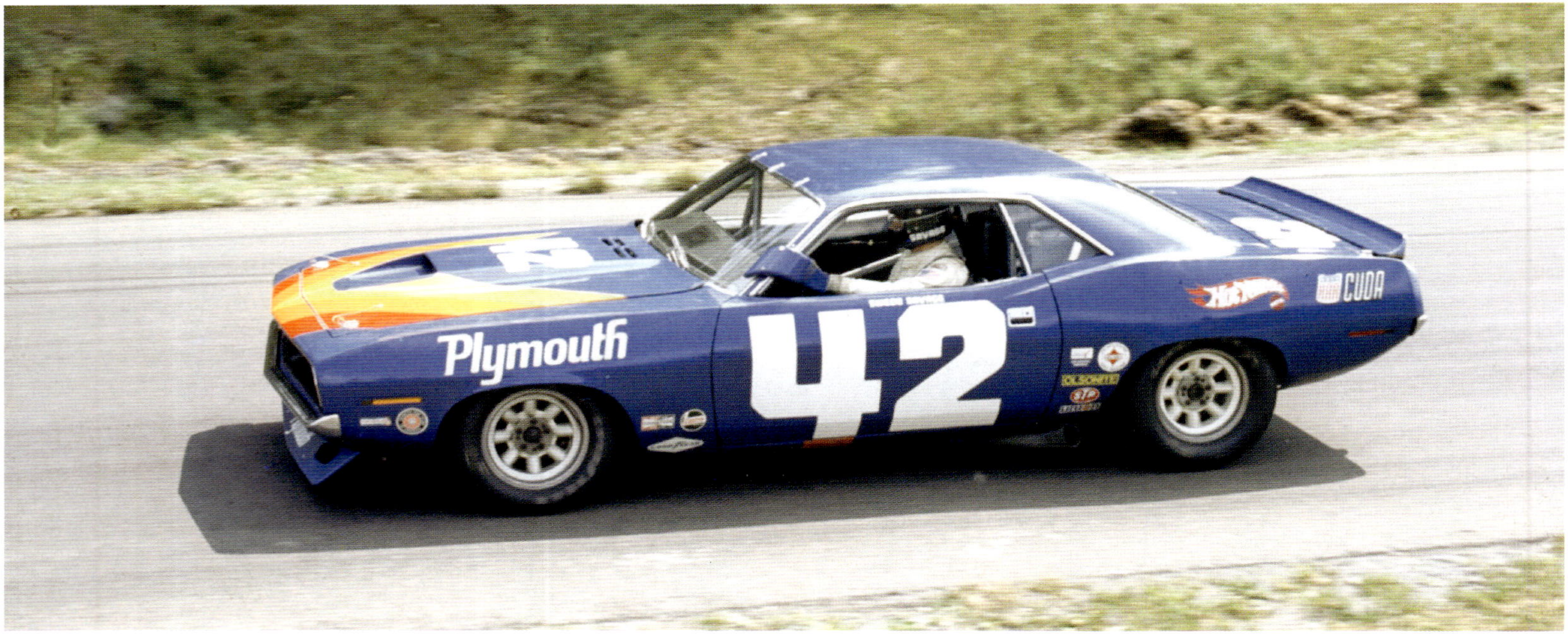
Plymouth
42
CUDA

Above: Gerald Robinson contested the Circuit Mont-Tremblant Trans-Am in his 1968 Barracuda. His race lasted until lap 45 (of 70). Jacques Duval gives chase in the second of the Todco cars, a 1969 Camaro. Allen Hewitt is next in the 1967 Camaro. (Courtesy Autosportsltd.com)

Top left: Savage and Revson scrap over the minor places after cresting the hill just past the pits. The Cuda has already hit something and knocked the front spoiler out of shape. (Courtesy Autosportsltd.com)

Left: Savage presses on in the Cuda. (Courtesy Autosportsltd.com)

Ron Kaplan Engineering

Although AMC assigned its Trans-Am Javelin program to Penske Racing for 1970, Ron Kaplan still played a role in the series. West Coast racer Ted Roberts received sponsorship from Norris Industries for a Trans-Am campaign, so contacted Kaplan about running a Javelin for him.

Kaplan still had one of the three factory cars from 1969, so updated it with 1970 sheet metal for Roberts, who almost ran the full schedule missing only the Riverside season-opener, and Donnybrooke.

Pontiac Firebird

The brand-new second-generation Chevrolet Camaro and Pontiac Firebird were launched on 26 February 1970. They were supposed to hit the market in September 1969, but a slew of delays pushed that back by five months.

The Camaro and Firebird were much the same car in design and construction. But the pair had quite different styling. John DeLorean, head of Pontiac division, insisted the two be different, so each would have its own identity. In fact, this insistence ensured that almost no sheet metal was interchangeable. But this in turn drove up development costs, and prevented other body styles, such as a convertible, from being introduced, because all the sheet metal needed changing, which was enormously expensive.

The Camaro and Firebird continued with a 108in wheelbase, but were 2in longer, 0.4in wider, and 1.1in lower than the first-generation models. The track was widened to 61in and the body was more rigid, while the steering

Above: Ed Leslie's Circuit Mont-Tremblant race ended abruptly, and painfully, with brake failure in his Chaparral Camaro. Donohue speeds past. (Courtesy Autosportsltd.com)

Opposite top: Roberts pits his Javelin. He finished 12th. (Courtesy Autosportsltd.com)

Opposite bottom: Posey, on full song in the Challenger, and executing a beautiful four-wheel-drift. (Courtesy Autosportsltd.com)

linkage was moved from behind the front axle to ahead of it, which was better for racing.

The second-generation Firebird featured a special beak with the twin grilles first introduced on the first-generation model. And like the 1969 Firebird, the nose would be an integrated Endura unit that blended effortlessly into the body, with little in the way of chrome embellishments. At the rear, the four slatted tail lights again defined this as part of the Pontiac family.

The Firebird and Camaro featured quite different wheel opening

treatment, with the Firebirds being more rounded. According to Pontiac designer Jerry Hirschberg, even the doors differed between the two models.

In addition to the base Firebird, Pontiac customers could tick their way up the options list to the Esprit, Formula and, at the top of the heap Trans-Am.

The Trans-Am was, as per its older sibling, Pontiac's homologation model for the SCCA Trans-Am series, and sported several trinkets that would be carried across to the race cars. Firstly, it had a functional reverse facing ram-air intake scoop (quickly dubbed a shaker hood), which popped up through a hole in the hood. The scoop sat atop a sealed shroud that wrapped around

After his early pit stop, it was a lonely race for Donohue. But that was just fine. As the competition were all beating each other up and wearing out their equipment, he just sped around quietly on his own, almost unnoticed. (Courtesy Autosportsltd.com)

Revson and Vic Elford push their equipment hard. In the end, the #9 Javelin came home fifth, while the Camaro retired with an electrical fault. (Courtesy Autosportsltd.com)

the carburetor, feeding cool air to it at the optimal location: the base of the windshield. This was another Herb Adams innovation.

There were also 'wheel opening air spoilers', the front sections of which blended neatly into a chin spoiler. The front fenders featured functional air extractors, designed to allow hot air from the engine bay to escape. At the rear was a tall three-piece deck spoiler, the main center section of which attached to the deck lid, while two corner caps were affixed to the tops of the rear quarters and remained in situ when the truck was opened.

With the new SCCA minimum build numbers for 1970 implemented, Pontiac had to produce around 3200 Trans-Ams, a tall order given that less than 700 versions of the 1969 model sold. It almost didn't happen. The Pontiac sales department didn't think 3200 Trans-Ams could find buyers. But Pontiac general manager F. James McDonald put his weight behind the program, and told the sales department they'd need to figure out a way to sell the model, because he was green-lighting it for production regardless.

All 3200 Pontiac Trans-Ams were painted either polar white with a single blue stripe down the center, or Lucerne blue with a single white stripe down the center. The shaker scoop was painted the same color as the stripe. 1970 was the first time the 'Fire Bird' emblem appeared on the model. Compared with the outlandish full hood decals that would epitomize the model within a few years, the 1970 edition featured a tasteful small single color flaming bird on the nose, just fore of the stripe.

The tiny T/G Racing team entered its second Trans-Am season in 1970 with the new second-generation Firebird. While even the Chrysler teams were funded around $1 million for their programs, which was less than Ford and AMC were tipping in, Pontiac reportedly paid T/G Racing around $200,000. So while all the factory teams were enjoying manufacturer support, the level of that support varied wildly.

But despite the piddling budget (relatively speaking), and the somewhat fragmented team arrangement (Jerry Titus and his crew were based in

The two factory Mopars going at it. Posey finished fourth. Savage didn't finish. (Courtesy Autosportsltd.com)

California, Terry Godsall in Canada, and Pontiac in Michigan), the T/G Racing crew produced a brilliant race car for 1970. Or, at least, the chassis was.

T/G Racing ultimately built three Firebirds for the 1970 season, even though the plan at the outside was to just race one. The first car arrived at the shop in December 1969. Remember, the second-generation Firebird didn't go on sale until February 1970, so donor cars for the racing program were in short supply. The first car was a Pontiac engineering test mule, whose main purpose was to serve as a template for the two cars that followed. When these finally arrived in March (the first championship race was in April!), the team had to scramble to make the opening event. But because everything had already been designed into the test mule, it was just a case of replicating that for the race cars.

The T/G Firebirds featured several innovative ideas. Firstly, they were fitted with variable-ratio power steering, running off a hydraulic pump. With Trans-Am races being quite long in duration, and the tires now getting so wide, power steering would help minimize drive fatigue as the race progressed. And because they'd already installed a hydraulic pump for the steering, they also ran hydraulic-assist power brakes.

Because of the power steering, T/G Racing was the only team in 1970 to successfully run its cars with larger rear tires on the front. Most teams ran a narrower tire there. This gave the Firebirds superb turn-in. T/G used Airheart disc brakes, which were also thought to give the factory Firebirds the best stopping power of all the Trans-Am cars in 1970.

Pontiac engineers Herb Adams and Paul Lamar helped design the suspension layout, which included a Watts-link in the rear, and the team used a full floating de-cambered rear axle, with one degree of negative camber, which was achieved by 'gronking' the rear axles. Two degrees of negative camber and eight degrees of caster was used in the front, and Titus liked to have huge anti-roll bars so the car cornered flat.

Pontiac engineers had developed the huge three-piece rear spoiler for the Trans-Am, which Chevrolet was forced to copy when its small deck spoiler, similar to that of the first-generation Camaro model, proved inadequate. But the late arrival of the second-generation GM pony cars had a knock-on effect, ensuring the big rear spoilers weren't approved until May 1970, which meant the Firebird and Camaro were forced to contest the opening event at Laguna Seca without them. Because they were bereft of rear spoilers, the front

Penske Racing had pulled this trick in the previous race at Road America of pitting Donohue early to get him out of the traffic. It worked there, and he won. And it worked again in Canada. (Courtesy Autosportsltd.com)

Top left: After losing its leader, the brilliant Jerry Titus, when he crashed in practice at Road America, the T/G Racing team returned to the Trans-Am at Watkins Glen with a new Firebird, wearing a new livery, and being driven by John Cordts. (Courtesy Autosportsltd.com)

Above: Donohue battled Parnelli Jones during the early part of the Watkins Glen race, until it rained. Then Vic Elford surged to the front in the Chaparral Camaro, and although Donohue closed in when the rain stopped and the track dried, Elford was still leading when the flag fell on lap 91. (Courtesy Autosportsltd.com)

Left: Posey rounds the final corner at Watkins Glen in the Autodynamics Challenger. His race ended with a DNF. (Courtesy Autosportsltd.com)

Top left: The Todco team traveled to Watkins Glen with the Firebird for Derek Johnson, but much like its home event at Circuit Mont-Tremblant, this was to be a short-lived race. Johnson went out on lap eight. (Courtesy Autosportsltd.com)

Bottom left: Cordts heads one of the Bud Moore Mustangs and a Chaparral Camaro onto the start/finish straight at Watkins Glen. The little T/G team was hoping for a good result, but sadly the Firebird stopped 13 laps short of the finish. (Courtesy Autosportsltd.com)

Dramatic image of Swede Savage in the AAR Cuda. He finished sixth at Watkins Glen. (Courtesy Autosportsltd.com)

Top right: American Motors supplied one of its new second-generation 1971 Javelins to be the pace car at Riverside, the final race of the 1970 Trans-Am. A total of 35 cars took the start, and although nobody could foresee it at the time, The Trans-Am would never be this good again. In an effort to score a race victory in the hopes of having their contracts renewed for 1971, AAR and Autodynamics raced two cars here. Gurney had come out of retirement, and Autodynamics completed its second Challenger shell. Tony Adamowicz drove the second Challenger. T/G Racing also had a second Firebird at this event. David Hobbs and Jerry Thompson were the two drivers. (Courtesy Autosportsltd.com)

Bottom right: An exciting first-lap scrap between the top factory cars, as Jones leads Follmer, Donohue, Gurney, Savage, Elford, and Revson. (Courtesy Autosportsltd.com)

spoilers also had to be removed to try to find some car balance. Both new GM pony cars looked a little bald as a result.

But if T/G Racing produced possibly the sweetest chassis on the grid with the smallest budget, the Pontiac motor that powered the Firebird failed it miserably.

After the ill-fated 303in³ tunnel-port head Pontiac motor had been abandoned in 1969, a more conventional approach was taken for 1970. Unfortunately, Pontiac really didn't have a suitable motor for the Trans-Am, even with the new engine regulations. The 400in³ unit was used as the basis for the Trans-Am effort, using the standard 4.25in bore combined with a 2.84in stroke to give 303in³ But the de-stroked 400 was heavy! It weighed around 100 pounds more than a small-block Chevy, but the cylinder heads didn't breathe as well, so it suffered the indignity of being both heavy and underpowered.

It was also unreliable. With massive 3.25in main bearings (the small-block Chevy had 2.25in mains), the Pontiac mill suffered from oil starvation. As a fix, engine builder Al Bartz tried mating conventional cylinder heads to the block used for the tunnel-port units, which had a deck height 1in lower than stock, and smaller main bearings. It was also lighter. The team arrived at the opening Trans-Am race with one of these motors fitted, and eagle-eyed SCCA tech inspector John Timanus immediately recognized it as a low-deck unit. As it wasn't a production motor, and not built in sufficient numbers, he advised the team to have the correct tall-deck motor in for the next race – or not bother showing up.

The little T/G Racing team struggled for the first half of the season,

This page: Posey chased down Revson, and ran close for a few laps, until, heading into the esses, the rear end of his Challenger broke away, and he spun through the dirt and dust, taking the Javelin driver with him. 'Revvie' was not amused. (Courtesy Autosportsltd.com)

blowing motors with alarming regularity, but the situation got much worse at Road America. During Saturday practice, Jerry Titus crashed into a bridge abutment after steering failure. It took him 17 days to succumb to his injuries. The team was built around Titus, who was universally loved. His crew were hugely dedicated to him, and now their leader was gone. Terry Godsall ultimately moved the operation to Canada, and ran two cars throughout the final races, but sadly, the results only got worse.

1970 Trans-Am

After two years playing bridesmaid to Chevrolet, Ford finally returned to the top of the Trans-Am Manufacturers' Championship in 1970. Of the six nameplates taking part, only three actually scored race victories.

Although Ford cut back on its funding to support just one team in 1970, it was clear from the outset the Bud Moore Mustangs were going to be hard to beat. The first-generation Mustang, as a platform, had been raced since 1965.

The two AAR Cudas battle Donohue early on. He'd get by both, but still finished third behind the Bud Moore pairing. Savage was fourth, Gurney fifth. This was to be Gurney's last race before retiring. (Courtesy Autosportsltd.com)

The Boss 302 motor was one of the most powerful in the field, and the Bud Moore crew – and its drivers Parnelli Jones and George Follmer – were largely unchanged from 1969. They were a polished unit.

By comparison, every other factory team in 1970 was either new to the manufacturer they were working with (Penske Racing), had a completely new product to work with (T/G Racing), or were new to the Trans-Am (AAR, Autodynamics, and Chaparral Cars). The Bud Moore team was the only one to enjoy continuity from 1969.

And so it panned out. Jones qualified fastest in the season opener at Laguna Seca, and Follmer was third. Splitting them was Donohue in the Penske Javelin. That's how they finished.

Gurney qualified in fourth position in the leading AAR Cuda, followed by Posey in the Challenger, and Ed Leslie in the lead Chaparral Camaro. Next was Titus in the T/G Firebird, and Savage in the second of the AAR Cudas.

From some perspectives, Penske Racing did well to finish second with a brand-new car and new manufacturer. But when the checkered flag waved after 90 laps, Jones was 40 seconds ahead of Donohue. In fact, Jones pulled away at the start, but dropped behind the Javelin after the pit stops. However, he simply caught and passed Donohue and drove away. Penske Racing knew it had work to do, but didn't know how to bridge the horsepower gap.

However, Penske was still doing better than the others. Savage worked his way up to fourth at the end, but was a lap behind Jones. Posey was three laps behind. Titus, four! But at least he finished. Gurney blew a transmission, and Revson, who'd started down the grid, retired with suspension failure.

Round two of the championship at the new Dallas complex was canceled after a massive rainstorm flooded the track. For T/G Racing and Chaparral Cars, this was a blessing in disguise because they could finally fit their big rear spoilers for Round three at Lime Rock in May.

The extra time gifted to the teams with the Dallas cancellation appeared to have benefited Penske Racing, as Donohue qualified on pole at Lime Rock in the lead Javelin, with Gurney lining up alongside. Jones and Leslie were next, followed by Savage, Revson, Follmer, Titus, Hall, and Posey. It was an impressive sight with the first five rows filled with factory cars representing all the major American manufacturers.

From the rolling start, Jones quickly disposed of Donohue and powered his way straight to the front, while Gurney slipped down the field. At the end of the first lap, Jones headed Donohue and Leslie. Donohue kept within striking distance of the flying yellow Mustang, until the AMC motor popped on lap 72.

Leslie finished a full lap behind in second place, after having to make an unscheduled pit stop when the Chaparral crew didn't replace his fuel cap during a scheduled stop. Such was the speed advantage Jones enjoyed, he nursed his car to the finish with no front brakes and a broken pushrod but still won by a lap.

Posey finished third, three laps behind at the finish, while Hall was fourth in the second Chaparral Camaro.

Titus retired with a fuel leak, while Follmer, Revson, and Savage all suffered the same fate as Donohue. Dry-sump oil systems couldn't come soon enough to the Trans-Am. Gurney retired with a blown clutch.

In between the Lime Rock race and the next Trans-Am event at Bryar, AAR reduced its commitment to a single-car team, following budget cuts enforced by Chrysler. Gurney decided he'd be the one to step aside, and Savage continued as a single-car team. At Bryar, he switched to Gurney's Cuda.

However, Savage showed just how much potential the Plymouth had, by qualifying on pole, with Jones starting alongside. Posey was third fastest, followed by Donohue.

In the end, Follmer surged through to take his first Trans-Am win of the season after Jones' hood blew off and he was black-flagged while leading. Revson finished second, ahead of Donohue. Both were three laps behind Follmer at the finish!

The fate of pole-man Savage, plus Titus and Posey, was worse still, as none of them finished.

Mid-Ohio hosted the next event on June 7, and although Donohue qualified fastest, Jones and Follmer simply powered past on the opening tour, and were never headed. Donohue finished third. At least he was on the lead lap this time. At least he finished! Most of the factory cars didn't. Savage suffered an oil leak, and Titus blew another motor.

From four races, Ford was seemingly untouchable.

The sweeping, high-speed dusty track in the sand dunes of Bridgehampton was next. Revson had other commitments, so Penske ran just a single Javelin for Donohue.

Savage again grabbed pole in the sole AAR Cuda, with Donohue starting alongside him. The budget-strapped AAR team was limited in how much testing it could do between races, but took the number 48 Gurney car to Bridgehampton a few days before the race, to get in some miles and trial some new parts, with Savage at the helm. Chrysler had supplied the team with one of its latest racing transmissions from its NASCAR program, fitted with an aluminum center section.

To that end, Savage blitzed the field in qualifying, and drove away in the race. He built a massive margin in the opening stint, before making his pit stop just as it was starting to rain. The team serviced the Cuda and sent Savage on his way. And that was the last it saw of him until he returned to the pits sometime later – on a borrowed moped. The new transmission had failed when Savage made his enthusiastic getaway at the pit stop.

Meanwhile, the wet track canceled out the power advantage of the Mustangs, and Donohue drove superbly to bring American Motors its first Trans-Am race victory. In fact, he won by two laps!

Follmer was next, and then Jones. Posey and Titus both retired with mechanical problems.

Interestingly, representatives of American Motors had scheduled a meeting at the Penske shop for the week following the Bridgehampton event. As it transpired, Penske Racing was to be informed it was being fired, because it had yet to win a race and the season was already half over. So Donohue's fortunate victory in the rain came at the perfect moment, and literally saved the program.

Donnybrooke was next and, again, Savage scorched around in qualifying to put the Cuda on pole. Jones was second. Posey and Donohue were back on the third row. Revson's commitments were still required elsewhere.

Posey's stricken Challenger is parked in the dirt while the California smog smudges the air in a thick haze. When he got back to the pits, Posey was accosted by an angry Revson, and the pair ended up in a tussle on the ground. As the Riverside race wound down, so the curtain lowered on an era of factory sedan racing that would never be seen again. Ford won the 1970 Trans-Am Manufacturers' Championship and promptly withdrew its support, as did all but American Motors. (Courtesy Autosportsltd.com)

As the 20 cars went barreling past the starter's flag, Savage again surged ahead. He stayed in front for the first half of the race, until the transmission stuck in second gear. He dropped through the pack, eventually finishing fifth, three laps in arrears. At least he finished. Jones, Donohue, Titus, and Posey all retired. Engine failure took out the Firebird and the Javelin.

This race was famously won by Milt Minter in the second of the two Roy Woods Racing 1969 Camaros (Woods finished third). Minter and Follmer banged panels several times as Follmer recovered from an earlier delay. During one of these skirmishes, the Mustang spun. He ultimately finished second. Minter was the first independent driver to win a Trans-Am race since Bob Tullius way back at the start of the 1967 championship.

For the Elkhart Lake event at Road America on 19 July, T/G Racing debuted a new 'lightweight' Firebird, which the team was hoping would reverse its fortunes. With the underpowered, unreliable, heavy Pontiac motor being the cars Achilles heel, the team sought to improve performance by further improving the chassis, and seeking weight savings in other areas. Tragically, Jerry Titus crashed the new car in Saturday practice.

Meanwhile, tensions within the Autodynamics camp had been ramping up as the season progressed, with Posey's Challenger qualifying poorly and often failing to finish the races. The relationship between Posey and Caldwell reached a new low at Bridgehampton, when Posey asked for Carroll Smith to join the team to oversee the day-to-day operation, and race weekends. Smith had enjoyed some spectacular successes in racing, and was part of Ford's Le Mans program.

Smith joined the Autodynamics team from Elkhart Lake, and suddenly the Dodge Challenger became not only more reliable, but faster! By mid-season, there was a simmering rivalry between the two Chrysler factory outfits and, to this point, AAR was the clear leader.

The two Bud Moore Mustangs qualified on the front row at the fast Road America circuit, but all hell broke loose when Leslie jammed his Chaparral Camaro between them into turn one, resulting in Follmer crashing, and Leslie being black-flagged. Jones escaped and controlled the race until the making his first pit stop.

From there, Posey swept to the front, and led his first Trans-Am race of 1970 by a comfortable margin, until he too pitted. But in the end it wasn't Jones who won, or Posey. It was Mark Donohue.

Attempting to overcome the horsepower deficit that blighted the Javelin, the Penske team came up with one of its 'unfair advantages'. A total of 36 cars started the O2 race, and generally speaking they all made their pit stops at around the same time, meaning they all got in each other's way, tripping over one another in the cluttered pit lane, and slowing down their service times as a result. But Penske Racing pitted Donohue for the first time on lap ten. From there he drove around all day more or less on his own, before making a second stop also out of phase with the others, winning by 58 seconds from Savage's Cuda, and Posey's Challenger.

Everyone stood around after the race scratching their heads. How did Penske just do that?

The Canadian Trans-Am race at Circuit Mont-Tremblant took place two weeks after Elkhart Lake, with Jerry Titus was still fighting for his life in hospital. Understandably, T/G Racing didn't attend the Mont-Tremblant event.

During practice, the spectacular Savage went off course and rolled Gurney's Cuda into a ball, and the team had to scramble to prepare the second car (that with which Swede started the season).

Interestingly, although T/G Racing was absent, a new second-generation Firebird appeared for this race, run by the Canadian team Todco (owned by John Todds), which also took a 1969 Camaro in the same colors. Derek Johnson drove the Firebird, and Jacques Duval the Camaro. Todco contested the first three rounds of the 1970 Trans-Am with a 1969 Firebird driven by Craig Fisher. His best result was an eighth at Lime Rock. This car was one of the 1969 T/G Firebirds, on loan from Terry Godsall. Interestingly, it was powered by a 303in^3 Pontiac motor, and wore the correct 1969 Firebird bodywork. And like the Pontiac-powered T/G Firebird in 1970, it broke more than it finished, failing to go the distance at Laguna Seca and Bryar.

And like the Pontiac-powered T/G Firebird and the borrowed 1969 Pontiac-powered Todco Firebird, the Pontiac-powered 1970 Todco Firebird also struggled to be both competitive and reliable. Johnson qualified mid-pack at Circuit Mont-Tremblant, and the engine let go after three racing laps.

Mont-Tremblant, however, would prove a happy hunting ground for Mark Donohue and Penske Racing. Donohue started on the front row alongside Jones, and the Penske Javelin pitted on lap 14, using the same method that worked so successfully at Elkhart Lake. And after 70 laps, when the rest of the field got done beating the stuffing out of each other, Donohue again scampered around almost unnoticed, and was in front when it mattered. Follmer and Jones were second and third, and Posey enjoyed another strong race, finishing fourth. The returning Revson was fifth. Savage retired on lap 27.

Since the arrival of Carroll Smith at Autodynamics, the fortunes of the Dodge and Plymouth teams had done a role reversal.

Sadly, Jerry Titus succumbed to his Elkhart Lake injuries on the Tuesday following the Mont-Tremblant event.

Watkins Glen was next, and the Chaparral team took its first Trans-Am victory, saving face after Milt Minter won in Roy Woods' year-old independent Camaro at Donnybrooke. Vic Elford was driving the number 1 Chaparral Camaro in place of team owner Jim Hall, and won from fifth on the grid, aided by the rain. Jones and Donohue battled at the front during the first 30 laps, but the Chaparral machine proved to be web-footed, and while Donohue was closing in late in the race as the track dried, he ran out of laps.

Revson finished fifth, Savage sixth. Posey failed to go the distance.

T/G Racing returned, with its Firebird painted dark blue with green highlights, and driven by John Cordts. It broke on lap 78 (of 91) after running mid-pack. That was still better than poor Derek Johnson who, after clocking just eight laps at Mont-Tremblant, only managed five at Watkins Glen.

Seattle Raceway in Kent, Washington, hosted the penultimate round of the 1970 Trans-Am Championship. And as we were nearing the end of the season, so the factory teams were pushing the boat out to get their contracts renewed. AAR entered two Cudas for Savage and Gurney. The team built up the third shell, and Gurney funded the Seattle and season-ending Riverside races out of his own pocket.

T/G Racing showed up with two Firebirds; one for Cordts, and one for David Hobbs. Autodynamics arrived with two Challengers: Ron Bucknum joined Posey.

For the Chrysler teams, word filtered out that only one of them would receive funding in 1971, but to do so, they needed to win a race in 1970. The pressure was on.

The race result was all-too familiar. Parnelli Jones won from Mark Donohue. However, Sam Posey took his first podium of the season. Neither of the T/G Racing Firebirds finished. Hobbs was the first retirement, on lap eight. Cordts was disqualified for charging the battery in the pits when his car wouldn't start after a pit stop. Gurney suffered an engine failure on lap 13, while his team-mate suffered the same fate on lap 78 (of 90). Bucknum retired on lap 29.

It had been a long and arduous season for the factory Trans-Am teams. The competition was intense, and the stakes high. The Bud Moore team looked to be the only one enjoying itself. Ford had already wrapped up the Manufacturers' Championship. Penske Racing had a three-year contract with American Motors. For everyone else, the future looked uncertain beyond the Riverside finale.

Tony Adamowicz replaced Bucknum in the second Autodynamics Challenger, and Jerry Thompson replaced Cordts in the second T/G Firebird.

Qualifying for Riverside was true to form. Jones qualified fastest, Follmer sat beside him. Next came Gurney's Cuda and Donohue's Javelin, followed by Savage, Revson, Posey, Elford, Leslie, Milt Minter in the Roy Woods Camaro, Adamowicz, and Hobbs in position 12.

Just before race start, Dan Gurney announced it would be his last race. He was retiring from driving to focus on managing his team.

It was an impressive 35-car field that rumbled around on the pace lap, with wall-to-wall factory cars. Nobody knew it at the time, but the Trans-Am would never be that good again

It was to be a dramatic race, with Jones leading until he clipped a lapped car and spun down to ninth. His Mustang looked ready for the scrapheap, with barely a straight panel left but he muscled his way back through the field and won by nine seconds from Follmer, while Donohue was a further 29 seconds adrift in third.

Savage and Gurney finished fourth and fifth, the first time both AAR Cudas went the full distance. Back in ninth, David Hobbs made a rare finish for T/G Racing although the Pontiac lump in Thompson's Firebird broke on lap 14.

Posey ran into Revson and the pair went spinning off through the dirt. They both got going again, but Posey's motor blew on lap 20 and Revson was involved in another shunt; this time he was out. The pair had a fight in the pits afterwards.

Adamowicz produced a second retirement for Autodynamics when his engine broke on lap 64.

It had been a highly emotional end to the season. Tensions were high, and fuses short. By 1970, there was a lot to play for in the Trans-Am series. Manufacturers were tipping millions into their race programs, and they expected, and demanded, results. But with so much tough competition, it became harder to achieve those results. While Ford, American Motors and Chevrolet all won races, Dodge Plymouth and Pontiac didn't.

In truth, when the dust and sparks settled and everyone looked forward to 1971, the only team that was truly safe was Penske Racing. It was the only one with a guaranteed contract.

1971

What happened? The 1970 SCCA Trans-Am series concluded at Riverside Raceway on 4 October, and there were 12 factory cars among a 35-car grid. Ford, Chevrolet, Pontiac, American Motors, Dodge, and Plymouth were all represented, and all entered two cars each.

And yet, come the opening 1971 Trans-Am race at Lime Rock Park on 8 May, only American Motors remained standing. And more than that, Penske Racing, the AMC factory team, chose to campaign just one car, for Mark Donohue. So in effect, 12 factory cars started the last race of 1970, and just one factory car started the first race of 1971. In just seven months, the Trans-Am had apparently imploded.

The Ford Mustang had been the catalyst for the new pony car sector when it was launched in April 1964, purely because it generated so much interest, and set new sales records. This was a segment that was fresh and exciting. And different!

Ford's rivals immediately unleashed programs to produce their own Mustang variants, based on the Mustang's styling, dimensions, layout, price point, and options list. Because Ford chose to race the Mustang, every manufacturer producing a Mustang competitor had to do likewise. It was the perfect storm. But by 1970 the gloss has faded noticeably.

There were several attributing factors to the pony car decline. Ford sold more than 559,000 Mustangs in 1965, its first full year of production. By 1970, that figure had dipped to 191,000. Part of the slump was due to the Mustang now facing so much competition. Rival manufacturers were stealing its sales. In 1965, the Mustang had the market to itself. In 1970, it competed against the Chevrolet Camaro, Pontiac Firebird, AMC Javelin, Dodge Challenger, Plymouth Barracuda, and Mercury Cougar. And that was just the pony car market segment.

Also, a global gas crisis was looming. The government was ratcheting up pressure on manufacturers to shift away from promoting power and speed. Also, insurance premiums on performance cars had gone stratospheric. Plus,

Lime Rock Park hosted the opening round of the 1971 Trans-Am Championship, and the impressive new Penske Racing Javelin undergoes some pre-race maintenance. This was the only factory car to contest the championship this season. (Courtesy Raynald Bélanger Collection)

six years had passed since the Mustang first appeared, and buyers' tastes and requirements were changing. Indeed, the baby boomer generation the Mustang was originally crafted for was now older and had different life priorities.

As a result, manufacturers saw little value in bucketing millions of dollars into a racing program for vehicles within a market whose sales were

It rained for the Lime Rock race. From pole position, Donohue's race was straightforward. After his main rival Parnelli Jones was knocked out of the race on the first lap, all he had to do was stay away from the muddy grass. He won by five laps from the ex-Bud Moore Mustang of Tony DeLorenzo, seen here giving chase. (Courtesy Raynald Bélanger Collection)

in decline. The Trans-Am of 1970 was quite different to that of 1966, in which independent teams operating on threadbare budgets were winning most of the races. And the problem with racing, of course, is that marketing clout can only be realized if the product you're marketing is succeeding in its given field. All at once, the manufacturers realized that competing in the Trans-Am just wasn't that important after all, and therefore, didn't warrant the investment required to be competitive.

Dodge, Plymouth, and Pontiac took no race wins in 1970, and none of these manufacturers returned in 1971. But even if AAR or Autodynamics managed to sneak a victory, Chrysler was already going cold on its commitment to the Trans-Am, and for that matter, racing as a whole. It began making budget cuts in the early part of the 1970 championship. There was some talk late in the season that Chrysler may return in 1971 and support just one team, but this came to nothing.

So too for Pontiac. Jerry Titus was the glue that held everything together at T/G Racing, and it was Titus whom Pontiac wanted to partner with. With Jerry's tragic passing, so the Firebird Trans-Am racing program quietly disappeared.

Perhaps more surprising was Ford, which had just won the Trans-Am Manufacturers' Championship for the third time in 1970. But Mustang sales were going the same way as performance car sales as a whole. The Mustang received a sizable makeover for 1971, and became bigger and heavier. And as the first-generation model was nearing the end of its life, and as its Pinto-based second-generation replacement was to take on a quite different theme, Ford took the opportunity to bow out on a high.

Bud Moore Engineering still had a fleet of Boss 302 racers, and would enter the 1971 Trans-Am as a two-car program. Although the team built two new cars for 1971 from a pair of fresh shells, and they were both painted the same color as those of 1970, without Ford money, this would be a very different campaign.

And what of Chevrolet? Officially, it hadn't been in racing since 1963. Unofficially, the Penske Racing collaboration had proven useful in promoting the Camaro as a practical sports car and a genuine Mustang rival, but by 1971, sales had slowed. Chevrolet had enough on its plate dealing with workers'

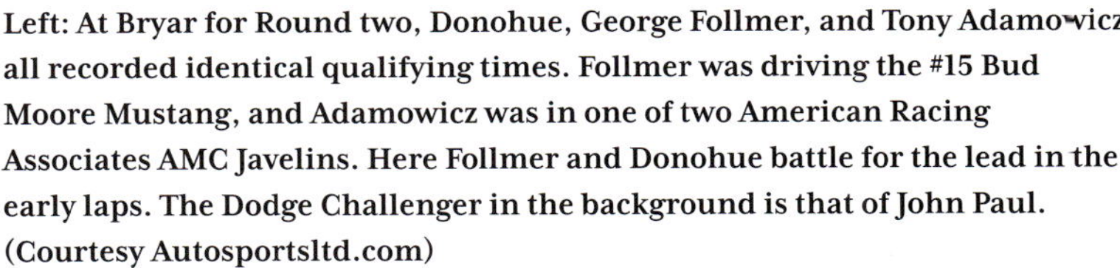

Left: At Bryar for Round two, Donohue, George Follmer, and Tony Adamowicz all recorded identical qualifying times. Follmer was driving the #15 Bud Moore Mustang, and Adamowicz was in one of two American Racing Associates AMC Javelins. Here Follmer and Donohue battle for the lead in the early laps. The Dodge Challenger in the background is that of John Paul. (Courtesy Autosportsltd.com)

Below left: An interesting addition to the 1971 Trans-Am Championship was this 1964 Pontiac Tempest, which was owned by Herb Adams. Despite appearances, it was a well-built car, designed and constructed by a small team of Pontiac engineers, and driven by Bob Tullius. Before becoming a race car, Adams' wife Sandy used the Tempest as her daily driver. Here at Bryar, Tullius finished a fine fourth position. (Courtesy Autosportsltd.com)

Opposite (clockwise from top left): The American Racing Associates AMC Javelin of Tony Adamowicz. This was one of two ARA Javelins run by Roy Woods. The other was driven here at Bryar by Peter Revson. These were 1970 Penske Racing Javelins, updated with second-generation 1971 sheet metal. (Courtesy Autosportsltd.com)

The 'Tire-Bird'. This T/G Racing-built 1970 Firebird was raced in the 1971 Bryar Trans-Am by Larry Dent, and was sponsored by BF Goodrich, which used it to promote its new range of radial street tires. In fact, it raced on radial street tires, albeit, not very competitively. Dent was last of the runners at Bryar. (Courtesy Autosportsltd.com)

With Ford having withdrawn its support at the end of 1970, Bud Moore Engineering carried on into 1971 as an independent team. Peter Gregg, pictured here, brought some desperately needed financial support. Here at Bryar, he finished second, while Revson, in the second ARA Javelin, was third. (Courtesy Autosportsltd.com)

Donohue chases Follmer during the early laps at Bryar. Despite now running a dry-sump, Donohue's engine failed at one-third distance, and Follmer went on to score a race victory for BME. (Courtesy Autosportsltd.com)

strikes and an increasingly challenging market. Going racing wasn't part of the equation. Jim Hall and his Chaparral Cars organization hadn't exactly dazzled. A single victory at a soggy Watkins Glen was all it had to show for its efforts. Sedan racing wasn't really Hall's thing, anyway. He was a sports car guy first and foremost. But even he had grown wary from the stresses imposed by years of intense competition. The SCCA had banned his radical Chaparral 2J 'sucker car' at the end of the 1970 Can-Am, and Hall vowed not to return. He was true to his word. And likewise, the Chevrolet Trans-Am program also reached its conclusion.

So that just left American Motors.

AMC Javelin

Penske Racing

Roger Penske stated during his public announcement in late 1969 that Penske

64

SUNOCO
Javelin
JAVELIN
GOODYEAR
PENSKE
BELL

6
AMX
Javelin
Javelin

PENSKE
6

Far left: John Paul raced this Dodge Challenger in the 1971 Bryar Trans-Am. It would be his only Trans-Am appearance this year. The Challenger was a former Autodynamics car from 1970. Dodge, of course, pulled the pin after just one season. Paul went out on lap 63 with low oil pressure. (Courtesy Raynald Bélanger Collection)

Left: The Penske crew pushes the magnificent new factory Javelin into tech inspection at Mid-Ohio. The second-generation Javelin was 1in longer in the wheelbase than the outgoing model, and several new body styling features were incorporated to assist with the Trans-Am program, including the sculpted front fender bulges, and mini spoiler at the rear of the roof. (Courtesy Raynald Bélanger Collection)

Bottom two photos: The Penske Javelin goes through tech inspection at Mid-Ohio. The second-generation Javelin featured a more pointed nose and protruded grille that both helped the race car cut through the air more cleanly at high speed. Penske opted for two separate chin spoilers made from Lexan which would flex slightly at speed, thus improving front downforce. The deck spoiler was based on the Don Cox-designed piece from the first-generation model, albeit, slightly taller. Attention to detail was always a Penske stronghold. Even the door gaps are as fine as can be to help the car move through the air cleanly. (Courtesy Raynald Bélanger Collection)

Racing would score seven Trans-Am victories in 1970 with the AMC Javelin. The reality was, Donohue won three races in a season dominated by Ford. But despite it all, Penske Racing and American Motors still emerged from the season looking like heroes. And what the team learned from campaigning the Javelin in 1970, and working to overcome its various frailties, would set it up nicely for 1971.

Of course, Penske Racing couldn't have known all its competition was withdrawing when it began developing the 1971 Trans-Am challenger. Penske opted to drop to a one-car team, with driver/engineer/developer Mark Donohue again taking a lead role. For the 1971 challenger, Penske Racing produced perhaps the best car of the entire 1966-1972 Trans-Am era.

In late 1970, American Motors launched its second-generation Javelin. It was, by all accounts, a very good-looking car, with styling features designed to encompass the Javelin's racing pedigree. The most prominent feature was the pair of sculpted front fender bulges. These were intended to accommodate large front racing tires with the nose set very low to the ground. Then there was the flush grille, to help with aerodynamics, and a

Top: The ARA Javelin of Tony Adamowicz in the Mid-Ohio paddock. Note the very different front spoiler to that of Penske Racing. (Courtesy Raynald Bélanger Collection)

Above: Although updated with 1971 sheet metal, it's likely the two ARA Javelins retained their 109in wheelbase, both being first-generation models. (Courtesy Raynald Bélanger Collection)

Left: ARA brought two cars to Mid-Ohio, and both went out within a lap of each other. Adamowicz crashed on lap 45, while Revson, pictured here, blew a motor the next lap. (Courtesy Raynald Bélanger Collection)

Bottom left: Mark Donohue, pictured in the yellow shirt, was having an easier time of it in 1971, with Penske Racing being really the only team with a completely new car, and certainly, the only team with factory support, and the best financial backing. That said, here at Mid-Ohio he was beaten by Follmer in the Bud Moore Mustang. This would be the last time he finished anywhere but first in the 1971 Trans-Am. (Courtesy Raynald Bélanger Collection)

Above, opposite and overleaf: The stunning Penske Racing Javelin rests in the pits at Circuit Mont-Tremblant. Attention to detail is apparent throughout. This was almost certainly the best car of the 1966-1972 Trans-Am era. Of course, when the Penske team began building this car, it wasn't to know all its rivals would withdraw. (Courtesy Denis Giguère)

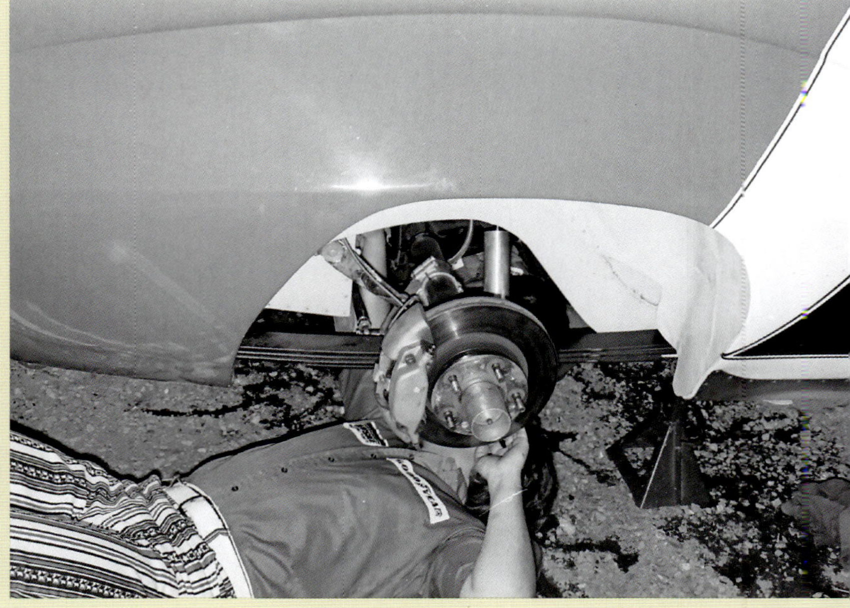

subtle spoiler molded in at the trailing edge of the roof. At the tail was the Don Cox designed rear-deck spoiler. There was also a front chin spoiler, although Penske Racing would create its own version for the race car, which was much deeper. Actually, the Penske Javelin sported two chin spoilers, positioned side by side. These were Lexan pieces which deformed at speed to provide more downforce the faster the car went, but which could also pass the SCCA minimum clearance test during tech inspection. Having two small spoilers rather than a single large one ensured replacement became easier. And replacements were required often, as Trans-Am cars were constantly whacking curbs and corner markers.

The second-generation Javelin was 1in longer in the wheelbase than the first-gen model, at 110in. With American Motors battling ongoing financial strain, it dropped the mad little two-seat AMX, which spanned 1968 through 1970. The AMX name-plate would therefore be carried across to the Javelin, so the 1971 Penske Racing Javelin was a Javelin AMX.

The SCCA changed little in the Trans-Am regulations for 1971. However, for the first time, dry-sump oil systems were allowed. Many might argue this rule change came two years too late. Certainly, the teams did.

The 1971 Penske Javelin was largely an improved, cleaner, more streamlined version of the 1970 car. Cox spent a lot of time developing adjustable front uprights, and Donohue wanted to ditch the brake booster setup for the sake of reliability. The team trialed twin-front calipers, but abandoned the concept early on.

One of the biggest areas for improvement was the motors. Traco Engineering had more experience with the AMC units, and the dry-sump system now offered some reassurance. A lot of development work went into the exhaust system, which resulted in an elaborate layout with four tail pipes (two on either side) running through channels cut into the floor. Nearly 50hp was gained through the exhaust system alone.

American Racing Associates

Meanwhile, American Racing Associates, the little enterprise owned by Roy Woods – who'd campaigned Camaros the last two seasons and surprised everybody by winning the 1970 Donnybrooke race – switched manufacturers to field a pair of Javelins in 1971. And these weren't just any Javelins. They were the two 1970 Penske Racing Cars, reskinned as second-generation models, and painted in the ARA racing colors of yellow and black. Woods already had a history with former Penske machinery. One of the Camaros his team raced in 1970 was an ex-Penske car.

Woods planned to drive one of his Javelins, but broke his foot in a Formula 5000 shunt, so the two ARA AMCs were driven for much of the season by Peter Revson and Tony Adamowicz. Vic Elford also had a turn, as did Milt Minter and George Follmer, who spent much of 1971 at Bud Moore Engineering. Follmer won Rounds two and three at Bryar and Mid-Ohio, joining ARA in the last race, when the cash-strapped BME opted not to travel all the way to California for the Riverside final.

Pontiac Tempest

Pontiac engineer Herb Adams had been instrumental in the T/G Racing factory Trans-Am program, and his involvement contributed to the Firebirds being some of the best handling cars on the Trans-Am grid in 1970.

But with Jerry Titus having died of injuries sustained at Elkhart Lake, so the glue that held the Pontiac Trans-Am program together came unstuck. Pontiac didn't so much make the decision to withdraw; the partnership just reached an end. However, Adams wanted to keep racing. He'd been bitten by the bug. He was working behind the scenes to run a Firebird in the 1971 Trans-Am with some financial assistance from Pontiac. But this ultimately came to nothing.

Quite by chance, however, Adams discovered that the first-generation Pontiac GTO had been homologated for racing back in 1965. The GTO was just a sporty version of the Tempest. By coincidence, Adams' wife, Sandy, just happened to own a 1964 Tempest she wanted to trade for something newer. Adams bought the Tempest brand new in September 1963, and later traded it to his dad for his mother to drive. He then bought it back again in 1968 for his wife.

The Tempest had already been warmed over a little before it was transformed into a Trans-Am car. Adams had fitted it with a roll cage, some racing wheels and tires, and used it for SCCA driver's school at Waterford Hills. He was aided in his SCCA club adventures by fellow Pontiac engineers Jeff Young and Tom Neil.

After victory in the Detroit News race at Waterford Hills, Adams decided to go all out and convert the Tempest into a Trans-Am racer. In all, he and six fellow Pontiac engineers (including Young and Neil) formed an incorporation, with each owing a percentage of the team, and thus, any prize and sponsorship money. Each team member was assigned an area on the car for which they were responsible.

Being a full-chassis car, the body was removed and the Tempest frame strengthened. Most Trans-Am cars used a parallel leaf-spring arrangement on the rear, but the Tempest had coil springs and a four-link as stock, which the team rebuilt and improved. Spring rates were relatively soft at 400lb in

Top left: It rained during practice for the Circuit Mont-Tremblant Trans-Am. The Herb Adams Tempest is pictured here, running steel wheels with its rain tires. With Tullius otherwise committed to a new Group 44 Triumph factory program, the Tempest was driven at Circuit Mont-Tremblant by Rusty Jowett. After busy campaigns in the 1968 and 1969 Trans-Am, Jowett was doing much less racing now. (Courtesy Denis Giguère)

Above: Roger Penske, pictured at Circuit Mont-Tremblant. (Courtesy Denis Giguère)

Left: The Penske Racing crew gathered in the pits at Circuit Mont-Tremblant with a selection of new and used tires. (Courtesy Denis Giguère)

This page and overleaf: Despite having won the last three Trans-Am races in a row, the Penske team never let its guard down. Here at Circuit Mont-Tremblant, it performs a practice pit stop with tire change. Roger Penske is the conductor. (Courtesy Denis Giguère)

Javelin
AMX
Javelin
Javelin

The relaxed-looking Penske Racing operation in the Circuit Mont-Tremblant paddock. (Courtesy Denis Giguère)

the front, and 200 in the rear. The Tempest used the Delco-Moraine Corvette-based disc brake package originally developed for the Trans-Am Camaro.

A Pontiac 389 HO block was used as the basis for the motor, onto which were fitted Ram Air IV heads. The blocks were acid-dipped to shed weight. Jeff Young built the Pontiac motors for the Tempest and, using the 4.125in bore, a 2.84in Moldex crank gave 303in^3. Young was able to extract close to 480hp from his Pontiac units.

Adams approached his friend Bob Tullius about driving the Tempest. Tullius wasn't convinced at first, but agreed to a test drive. When he first saw it, the Tempest was painted purple and green, and he told the team if he was to race it, the color had to change. Eventually, it was finished in silver, and garnered the nickname 'Gray Ghost'.

Tullius brought in sponsorship from Quaker State and Classic Wax, which allowed the little team to attend most races on the 1971 Trans-Am schedule.

BOAC 747
839-85P

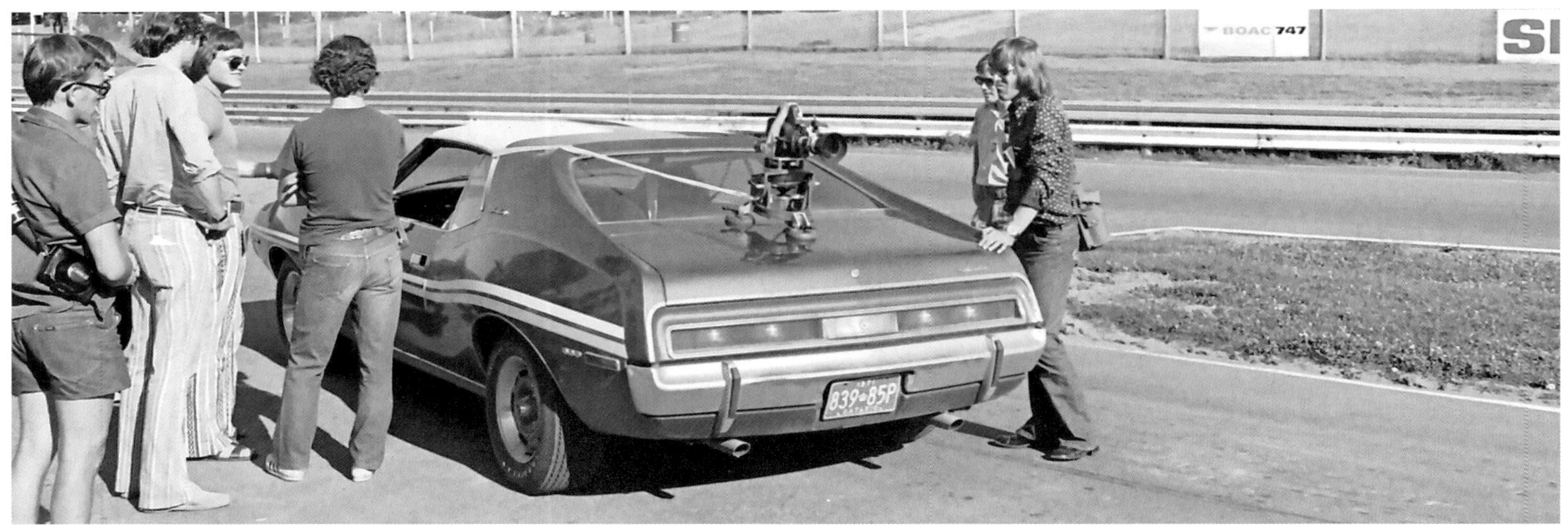

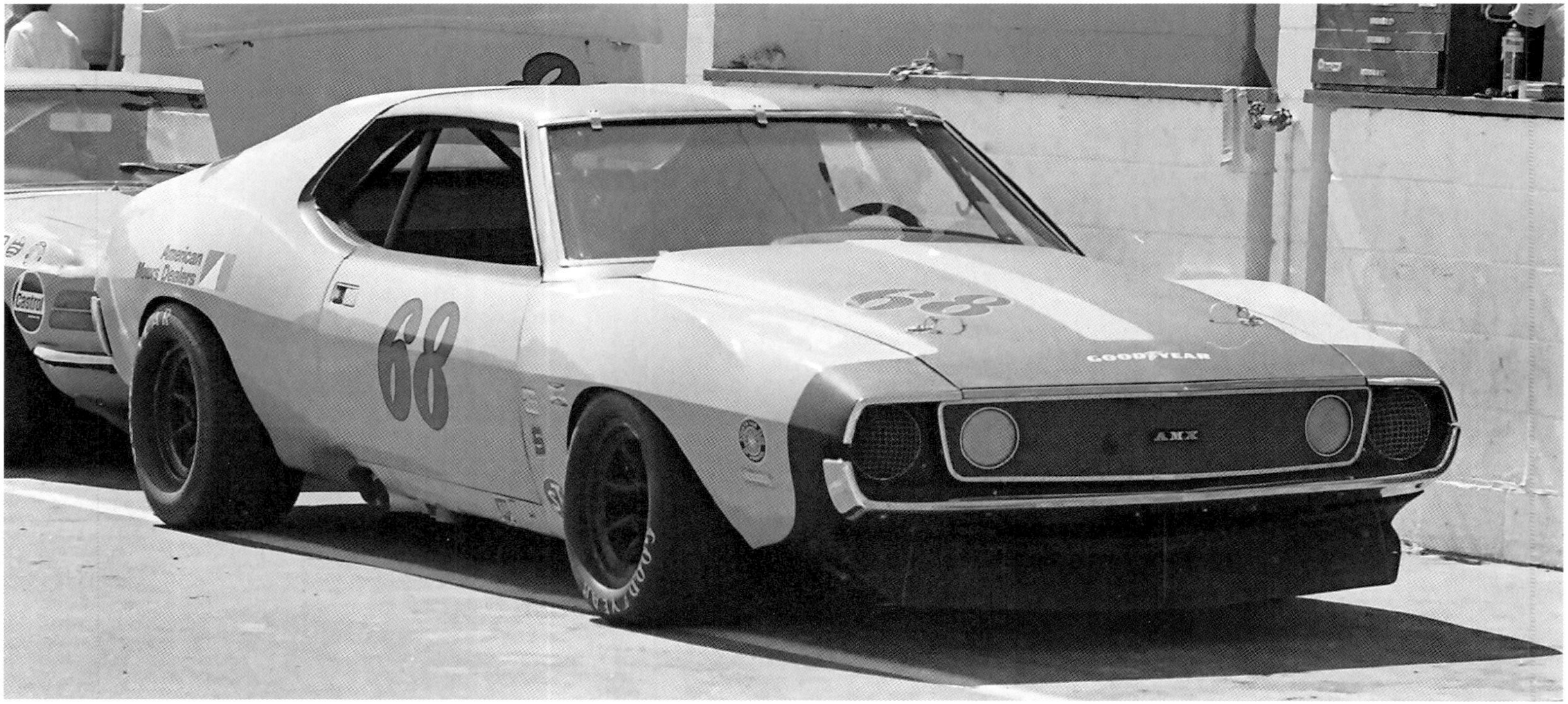
American
Motors Dealers
Castrol
68
68
GOODYEAR
AMX

Opposite top: AMC Javelins were used as pace cars for several Trans-Am races in 1971. This one is rigged up to film the pace lap. (Courtesy Denis Giguère)

Opposite bottom: Revson's ARA rests in the Circuit Mont-Tremblant pits. He qualified third behind Donohue and Follmer. (Courtesy Denis Giguère)

Below: A dramatic rolling start for the 1971 Circuit Mont-Tremblant Trans-Am as the field dives into the first turn. Donohue and Follmer lead the charge, with the two ARA Javelins giving chase. (Courtesy Denis Giguere)

RRIVÉE
FINISH
RENAULT
FABRIQUE
AU
CANADA

Clockwise from far left: Revson throws his Javelin into turn one, with Peter Gregg's BME Mustang in hot pursuit. (Courtesy Denis Giguère)

The top four were this close at the end of lap one. Note how flat the Penske Javelin corners compared with the ARA variant in third. (Courtesy Denis Giguère)

Milt Minter drove the second ARA at Circuit Mont-Tremblant. Here he battles Marshall Robbins in his self-built Camaro, a partially built Chaparral factory car from 1970 that Marshall and his crew completed for the 1971 season. Marshall finished seventh, while Minter had an engine let go. (Courtesy Denis Giguère)

Donohue charges back into battle after being dispatched by his crew following a pit stop. His would be a closely fought battle throughout with Follmer. (Courtesy Denis Giguère)

Jowett qualified the Tempest in position 23, but his race ended early with a blown motor. (Courtesy Autosportsltd.com)

The Gray Ghost may have looked like a seven-year-old mid-sized grocery-getter, but it was, in every respect, a brand-new Trans-Am car, albeit one built to a very tight budget.

1971 Trans-Am

The 1971 SCCA Trans-Am Championship was shortened to ten rounds. Although most of the manufacturers had withdrawn from the O2 class, the U2 division grew in stature. The SCCA tweaked the U2 engine size formula, increasing it to a maximum of 2500cc and, with it, was rebranded as the Trans-Am Two-Five Challenge. The Two-Five Challenge very quickly became the healthiest segment of the Trans-Am, with manufacturer support from Datsun, Alfa Romeo and, to a lesser extent, BMW. Even Triumph got involved.

Thus, the Two-Five Challenge emerged from the shadows of the Over

Above: Donohue won his fourth race in succession in Canada. But he had to work for it. Follmer was always within striking distance. (Courtesy Autosportsltd.com)

Left: Lovely attention to detail on the Tempest as it rests in the grassy Michigan International Speedway paddock. Herb Adams and his team were able to build a Pontiac motor that, for the most part, held together in a road-racing environment. (Courtesy Larry J Honegger)

Left and above: Pace lap for the 1971 Michigan International Speedway Trans-Am. The track layout included a portion of the banked speedway and the infield, and this undulating section outside the speedway itself. Of course, a Javelin pace car was used. (Courtesy Paul Castagnoli)

2 class and, at Olathe Naval Air Station and Laguna Seca, had its own standalone events where the O2 cars weren't invited.

The 1971 Trans-Am Over 2 Championship started at Lime Rock on 8 May, followed by Bryar, Mid-Ohio, Edmonton, Donnybrooke, Road America, Circuit Mont-Tremblant, Watkins Glen, Michigan International Speedway, and concluded at Riverside on 3 October. It was clear from the outset how quickly the series had sunk.

Donohue qualified fastest, while Bud Moore worked a one-race deal to have Parnelli Jones drive one of his Mustangs (the other was driven by Peter Gregg, who brought finance to help fund the program). Next were the two ARA Javelins. Bob Tullius had to get special clearance to start the race from the rear of the grid when the Gray Ghost's clutch failed three laps into qualifying and he failed to record a time.

It rained heavily in the Lime Rock race, and after Jones was punted off on the opening tour (and promptly retired from road racing), Donohue drove

Left: The field bunches up as it winds around the MIS infield, getting ready to go racing. As was the case for much of the 1971 season, Donohue and Follmer shared the front row, while the two ARA Javelins locked out row two. On the fifth row can be seen Tullius in the Tempest. (Courtesy Larry J Honegger)

Top left: Donohue leads Follmer during the early part of the MIS Trans-Am. The pair finished in this order. Although not known at the time, this was to be Mark Donohue's last Trans-Am race. (Courtesy Paul Castagnoli)

Above: Tullius pushes hard around the MIS banking on his way to an eventual fifth place. (Courtesy Larry J Honegger)

Left: The two ARA Javelins in close formation. Milt Minter was back driving the 69 car at MIS. They finished in this order. (Courtesy Paul Castagnoli)

away from the field. Meanwhile, the wet track suited the softly sprung Gray Ghost, and Tullius slithered his way confidently through the field. By lap 100 (of 132), he was running second to Donohue, and gaining! Every lap he ran, the crowd got more excited, and treated him to a standing ovation every time he flew past. Could Tullius pull off the impossible and beat the mighty Penske Racing factory squad in Herb Adams' wife's ancient Tempest? No.

On lap 120, Tullius pulled into the pits with a blown head gasket. Adams tipped water into the radiator and sent him on his way, but the Tempest completed one slow lap (with the crowd still roaring!) and pitted again, for good. The team tried to coax the motor into life to complete the final lap and at least be classified a finisher, and collect a little prize money, but it wouldn't start. Had positions been rewarded for laps completed, Tullius would have taken eighth place. Instead he was classified as did not finish.

Donohue went on to win the Lime Rock race by five laps from Tony De Lorenzo's independent Mustang. Five laps!

For the Bryar race, George Follmer filled Jones' seat in the Bud Moore Mustang, and won the race! From the qualifying times, it looked as though this might be a classic, for Follmer, Donohue and Adamowicz all recorded identical times.

Donohue and Follmer scrapped over the lead until lap 34 when the Javelin's motor blew, and both drivers spun on the oil. Follmer got going again and was never headed. Gregg was second in the second Bud Moore Mustang, while Revson was third in the sole surviving ARA Javelin. Tullius was fifth in the Tempest, having started in tenth.

This race enjoyed some added interest among the sea of Mustangs and Camaros, with the addition of John Paul (Snr) in a Dodge Challenger, and Larry Dent in a Pontiac Firebird. Both cars were former factory racers from the 1970 season. Paul was aboard one of the Autodynamics Challengers, and Dent a T/G Racing Firebird. The Firebird was still being campaigned by T/G Racing, and sponsored by BF Goodrich Tires, which was promoting its new radial street tires by running them on the Firebird. Emblazoned down the side bodywork was the wording 'BFG Radial Tire Bird'. Incidentally, the team also campaigned a Camaro in 1971 which, confusingly, carried the same lettering. In the end, John Paul had oil pressure troubles and retired on lap 63, while the Tire Bird completed 83 laps on its street radials to be classified 16th, and last.

It rained at Mid-Ohio for Round three of the championship and, just like at Lime Rock, Tullius came surging forward in the Gray Ghost. He started seventh, and quickly worked his way to second, behind Follmer. He was catching, too, until the pit stops. Herb Adams and his crew of volunteers built a good car, but they were still volunteers working regular day jobs. They weren't a well-drilled, cohesive racing operation. While the Bud Moore crew serviced Follmer with four tires and fuel in less than a minute, Tullius was stationary for three minutes and 43 seconds.

After a spirited performance, Tullius worked his way back up to fifth at the end. Follmer won, from Donohue, who struggled with brake issues throughout. Neither of the ARA Javelins finished.

The little American Racing Associates team skipped the next race in Edmonton, Canada, as did Tullius and the Gray Ghost. Here Donohue won from Follmer, with both cars handicapped by engine dramas.

In the Donnybrooke race, Donohue and Revson battled for the lead throughout in their Javelins, and that's how they finished. The Bud Moore team opted to skip this race, due to lack of funding. Adamowicz and Tullius both retired with busted suspension.

Donnybrooke set in motion a run of race wins for Donohue and Penske Racing that also included Road America, Circuit Mont-Tremblant, Watkins Glen, and Michigan International Speedway, and with that, the 1971 Trans-Am Manufacturers' Championship finally went the way of American Motors Corporation.

Tullius finished fifth in the Michigan race, while the ARA Javelins either broke or finished just off the podium at most of the remaining events. However, Revson was third at Michigan, ahead of team-mate Milt Minter, making his first appearance of 1971.

Michigan would be the last appearance in the Trans-Am for the Herb Adams Tempest. The little team couldn't afford to travel to Riverside for the final. It would also be the last appearance for Mark Donohue. While Penske Racing made the long haul to California, Jackie Oliver drove the Javelin.

With Follmer at a loose end, he was plugged into one of the ARA Javelins, and promptly won the race! Team-mate Vic Elford finished second. Capping off an AMC clean sweep of the podium was Jackie Oliver.

The Riverside race featured some interesting local Trans-Am challengers, including the elderly Plymouth Barracuda of Bob Hampton, which retired on lap six, plus the Dodge Challenger of Dick Brooks, which retired on lap 12, and the AMC Javelin of Buzz Dyer, which retired on lap 32 (of 79). The Brooks Challenger was not one of the Autodynamics cars from 1970. Instead, it was an independent build, entered by motoring journalist and part-time Trans-Am racer Brock Yates. Buzz Dyer's Javelin was the former Ron Kaplan 1969 model that was raced throughout 1970 by Ted Roberts.

The Trans-Am may have lost almost all its factory teams in 1971, but the independents were keeping the series afloat.

The Penske team gets to work knocking out another super-slick pit stop. The car and crew look familiar, but the driver doesn't. Penske was contractually obliged to send the Javelin all the way to California for the Riverside final, but with the Manufacturers' Championship already sewn up, Roger couldn't see the point in Donohue also attending ...

... To that end, Swede Savage was asked to drive the Javelin. He agreed, but when a better offer to race a USAC car arose, he pulled out. So stock car racer Donnie Allison was approached, but he broke his hand on the steering wheel during practice when the Javelin hit a bump. So, finally, Jackie Oliver was asked to drive. He finished third. (Courtesy Bruce Stewart)

Above: The ever resourceful Vic Elford drove the #68 ARA Javelin at Riverside. He went on to finish second. (Courtesy Bruce Stewart)

Top right and right: The #69 ARA Javelin makes a pit stop in the Riverside Trans-Am. With the Bud Moore team low on funds, it opted not to travel to California. After all, the Manufacturers' Championship had already been won by AMC, and it meant nothing to BME, anyway. So George Follmer was without a ride. That was, until he was offered a seat in the ARA Javelin. He put the car on pole, and won the race. (Courtesy Bruce Stewart)

Follmer enjoys the celebrations after having won the Riverside Trans-Am.
(Courtesy Bruce Stewart)

1972

The end was near. The 1971 SCCA Trans-Am Championship was all one-way traffic. Penske Racing was the only factory team taking part, and won most of the races. But even if there had been a full fleet of factory racers like in 1970, Penske Racing might well have won the title anyway. That's how good it was. And that's how good the 1971 Penske Javelin was.

Following its rapid ascent, the Trans-Am quickly descended within the months that followed the 1970 championship, in which most of the manufacturers withdrew.

Although the SCCA originally intended that the Trans-Am be an Americanized version of the European Touring Car Championship, made up largely of independent teams and a broad spread of makes, models, and engine sizes, what it quickly evolved into was a V8 pony car war in which the American manufacturers waded in heavily. And with the manufacturers all waving money about, so the slew of international superstar drivers soon ascended, further raising the stakes and the spectacle. That the 1970 series was so stacked with factory machinery and professional drivers made everything that followed appear hollow by comparison.

The Trans-Am had truly soared to epic heights. Now its very survival looked in doubt. And it all happened so quickly.

The 1972 Trans-Am O2 Championship was reduced to just seven races, although this wasn't part of the original plan. Several event promoters canceled their races at the eleventh hour when they could see spectator numbers were plummeting. Without the factory teams and their superstar drivers, the fans had little appetite for the Trans-Am. To that end, the 1972 SCCA O2 Championship began at Lime Rock Park on 6 May, followed by races at Bryar, Mid-Ohio, Watkins Glen, Donnybrooke, Road America, and Sanair airstrip in Quebec, on 30 July. And that's where it ended.

If there was a silver lining, it was surely the Two-Five Challenge for small-bore sedans, which continued to grow, and boasted some quite impressive factory support.

Prize money increased modestly from the early days to $24,000 per race. The O2 race winner took home $4000, while second and third collected $3000 and $2500 respectively. Of the three professional road racing championships run by the SCCA (Can-Am, Formula A/5000, and Trans-Am), the Trans-Am was certainly the most miserly. Trans-Am sedans weren't cheap to buy or run. But then again, they were cheaper and easier to run than a Formula 5000, and certainly more so than a Can-Am car. And so, even though the factory teams were but a distant memory, O2 Trans-Am grids surpassed 30 cars for every race in 1972. Surprisingly, the series was enjoying record entries. And yet, the Trans-Am itself was on its knees.

From its inception in 1966, the Trans-Am had some of the best racing drivers on the planet. It was common to see Formula 1 stars strapping into a Trans-Am car when their commitments allowed. And yet, the SCCA decided to wait until 1972, when almost all the stars had left, to finally introduce a Trans-Am Drivers' Championship.

As had been the case in 1971, there would be just one factory team in the 1972 series: American Motors.

AMC Javelin

Although Penske Racing still had a year to run on its contract with American Motors Corporation, with ambitions far greater than a fast-fading SCCA Trans-Am, it saw little point in pummeling a handful of modestly funded privateers into submission for a second year running, and so passed the Javelin operation to Roy Woods, and his newly rebranded Roy Woods Racing. This was an agreement that worked for everyone; AMC retained a winning presence in the series, Penske was free to pursue other challenges, and after three seasons punching above their weight, Roy Woods' modest team scored itself a factory deal.

Fortunately, RWR ran two Javelins in 1972. These were actually the same cars it campaigned in 1971, which were the two original Penske Racing Javelins from 1970. One was driven by George Follmer, the other by Roy Woods.

Roger Penske, meanwhile, sold the 1971 Penske Racing Javelin to 21-year-old independent racer Bill Collins. Actually, it was Bill's dad who bought the Javelin. He just happened to own the Minnesota Fighting Saints hockey team, and the Javelin was used as a promotional vehicle.

Pontiac Firebird

Having won over a legion of fans with his charismatic 1964 Pontiac Tempest in the 1971 Trans-Am, Herb Adams and his partners built a new Pontiac Firebird Trans-Am for the 1972 series. Aside from the RWR and Bill Collins Javelins, the 1971 Trans-Am was packed with Mustangs and Camaros, of varying vintage. So the Adams Firebird offered some desperately needed contrast.

The Firebird was the only new car built for the 1972 Trans-Am, and carried over several of the lessons learned from running the Tempest. The Firebird was painted black, and sat very low to the ground, with the front wheel openings radiused out to make space for the latest big, sticky tires. Interestingly, the hood scoop was molded into the hood, rather than poking up through it as an engine attachment. Certainly, some testing would have shown this to be a better method for feeding the big Holley housed within it. It wore a pair of chrome number 0s on the doors, and rolled on Motor Wheel Spyders, an interesting alternative to the popular Minilites that most teams preferred.

Of course, being prepared by Pontiac employees, the Firebird was Pontiac-powered. It was fitted with a dry-sump, which massively aided reliability. Pontiac was said to have supported the program, but if money actually changed hands, it was a minimal amount, because Adams and his team operated on a budget of $1000 per race.

Bob Tullius was scheduled to drive the Firebird, but missed the opening race at Lime Rock due to a non-racing accident. Adams thus opted to drive the car himself but was four seconds off the pace, so the team asked Tony DeLorenzo to drive instead. From Round two on, however, Milt Minter took over driving duties.

1972 Trans-Am

George Follmer got his campaign off to the best possible start, by winning at Lime Rock from Warren Agor's Camaro, and DeLorenzo. Woods was fourth, and Collins seventh.

Follmer also won at Bryar, with Minter finishing second in the Adams Firebird, from Agor. Minter started the Bryar race from pole, while Follmer crashed in qualifying and was off the back. The Javelin worked its way through the 30-car field and eventually passed Milt for the win. As it transpired, Minter was driving ultra-conservatively, to save the equipment, and at least pick up $3000 for finishing second. It was all about the dollars and cents.

At Mid-Ohio for Round three, Minter made history by giving Pontiac its very first Trans-Am victory! Too bad Pontiac itself had long since withdrawn from the series, but the little Adams crew was delighted. Pontiac was still paying the SCCA $5 for every Trans-Am it produced, so scoring the first Trans-

Above: Remarkably, despite the ongoing decline of the SCCA into 1972, the grids were bigger than ever. At most events, more than 30 cars started. The trickle-down effect of all the factory involvement since the series began, and the money pumped into the series meant a lot of cars had been built. Of course, the only factory team still competing was American Motors which, much like 1971, won most of the races. (Courtesy Stu Brennan)

Righr: American Racing Associates rebranded itself as Roy Woods Racing in 1972, and thanks to its commitment running ex-Penske Javelins the year prior, was offered the AMC factory deal for 1972. Better yet, RWR ran two cars: one for George Follmer and one for Roy Woods. Here at Lime Rock, Follmer leads Warren Tope's Mustang, Maurice 'Mo' Carter's Camaro, Woods, and Alfie Ruz DePerez in another Camaro. The DePerez Camaro, run in partnership with lone-time Trans-Am racer Carter, was the Pontiac Firebird run as the BF Goodrich Tire-bird in 1971, but rebuilt as a Camaro so it could run a Chevy motor. (Courtesy Stu Brennan)

Opposite top: Although Roy Woods Racing took over the AMC factory program from Penske Racing, it didn't take over the 1971 Penske Javelin. Instead, it continued racing the same reskinned 1970-1971 Javelins campaigned the previous year. The 1971 Penske Javelin was sold and raced by Bill Collins and continued to wear its Penske livery until it was repainted blue and yellow. (Courtesy Stu Brennan)

Opposite bottom: After an encouraging season racing the charismatic Tempest, Herb Adams and his team built this very neat Firebird Trans-Am for the 1972 season. Milt Minter was the driver, and he scored a victory for the little team at Mid-Ohio. With the SCCA Trans-Am now in freefall, this was the only new car built for the 1972 season. (Courtesy Stu Brennan)

63
BILL COLLINS
Collins
RACING
GOODYEAR
DREW
AGENCY
96
EZ
HAUL

Am victory for a Pontiac Trans-Am was a historic moment, if largely overlooked by the manufacturer. Follmer was second, from Agor, Collins, and Woods.

It was situation normal at Watkins Glen, as Follmer took another win. However, this was only after Minter blew his motor while leading. This time it was Jerry Thompson who was second in a Mustang, from Woods.

At Donnybrooke, Follmer took his fourth win from five starts, while Thompson was again second, and Woods third. Minter placed fourth.

Follmer qualified on pole at Road America in the RWR factory Javelin, but the motor popped on lap 39 of 50. Warren Tope, in a Mustang, collected the race win from Minter and Collins.

Despite Follmer going out early in the Road America event, he'd accumulated enough points to be uncatchable, and won the first SCCA Trans-Am Drivers' Championship. And that might have been the highlight of his 1972 racing season had he not also won the 1972 SCCA Can-Am Championship. The Can-Am wasn't part of his schedule at the start of the year. However, following the first round of the series at Mosport Park, Mark Donohue pirouetted the wicked new twin-turbocharged Penske Racing Porsche 917/10 in testing, smashing his left leg. Penske Racing rebuilt the car and invited Follmer to drive it for the remainder of the series. He won on debut in Round two, beating the previously dominant factory McLarens which had owned the Can-Am since 1967, and he ultimately went on to win the 1972 Championship, becoming the only driver to win both the Trans-Am and Can-Am Championships in the same year.

To that end, Follmer didn't drive the RWR Javelin in the Sanair final. He was racing a Formula 5000 at Donnybrooke instead. His seat was taken by Baja off-road racer Bob Ferro. However, after practice, Woods was highly unimpressed by the rough Sanair track and promptly withdrew both his cars.

The Sanair race was won by Tope, from Collins, and Paul Nichter in a Camaro. Minter went out on lap five with a blown motor.

So it was that Follmer became the inaugural SCCA Trans-Am Drivers' Champion. Despite missing the first race, Minter finished second. For what it's worth, American Motors Corporation won the Manufacturers' Championship, with Ford second, and Pontiac third. Of course, AMC was the only manufacturer still taking part in an official capacity.

With that, the 1972 Sports Car Club of America Trans-American Sedan Championship drew to an unspectacular, unplanned conclusion, and its very future looked in doubt. Also, after the withdrawal of the two RWR Javelins, the final race of the original 1966-1972 Trans-Am featured no factory cars for the first time in its history.

Although nobody knew it at the time, including the SCCA, the lackluster Sanair event, in which only nine of the 27 starters were still circulating at the end, would be the last race of the original Trans-Am era.

1973 and beyond

Remember that guy John Bishop who'd been instrumental in creating the Trans-Am series during his stint at the Sports Car Club of America? He left in 1968 when the SCCA started fiddling with the FIA Group 2 Touring Car rules the series was originally built on.

But he hadn't spent the intervening years sat on a beach. Instead, he established an entirely new racing body called the International Motor Sports Association (IMSA).

IMSA made a humble debut in 1969. There was a single race at Talladega Super Speedway for imported small-bore touring cars. It was won by Gaston Andrey in an Alfa Romeo GTA. Two of the entrants were Bill France Snr and Bill France Jnr, owners of the National Association for Stock Car Auto Racing (NASCAR), and of the Talladega facility the race was being contested at. The Frances each drove a MkII Ford Lotus Cortina, but there was more to it than that. Bill France Snr also owned a 25 percent stake in IMSA.

In 1970, IMSA expanded to two events, again for small-bore touring cars, with races at Summit Point and Montgomery Speedway.

In 1971 there was a change of tack, with the introduction of production GT sports cars using FIA Group 4 regulations, but under the guise of GTU (for cars up to 2500cc), and GTO for GT cars over 2500cc. Also, the touring car division was expanded to two classes, for cars up to and over 2500cc. There were six races, at Virginia International Raceway, Talladega, Charlotte Motor Speedway, Bridgehampton, Summit Point, and Daytona International Speedway. Each of the speedway events was contested on the road course layouts.

Until this point, it had all been pretty modest, and no doubt even the SCCA wasn't taking IMSA too seriously. But that all changed for 1972 when Bishop and France sweet-talked R J Reynolds into sponsoring the championship with its Camel cigarettes brand, to the tune of $300,000. Indeed, Reynolds had recently started sponsoring the NASCAR Grand National in 1971 with its Winston brand, thus the long association as the NASCAR Winston Cup began.

Suddenly, the newly branded IMSA GT Camel Series became a road racing powerhouse. The 1972 championship featured eight rounds, and boasted a fascinating variety of machinery, from Trans-Am cars to Porsche 911s, including a semi-factory supported team from Brumos, as well as Corvettes and De Tomaso Panteras and Mangustas. The spread of race winners was equally compelling. Ford Mustang, Chevrolet Corvette, Porsche 911, and Chevrolet Camaro all rolled into the victory lane at various times during the year.

In 1973 the IMSA GT Camel Series got bigger still, particularly as a result of hosting the Sebring 12-Hours. And because of its rich prize purse, a great many independent SCCA teams converted and updated their old Trans-Am machinery to suit the IMSA regulations. Unlike the Trans-Am, IMSA had no maximum engine size, and therefore, a glut of teams campaigning second-generation Camaros repowered their cars with big-block motors. Likewise, there were no limitations on wheel sizes, and so the old Trans-Am racers morphed into menacing hulks with massive wheels housed inside broad fender flares. Some of the transformations were neatly done. Some looked dreadful. But IMSA offered these car owners a new, more richly rewarding platform to keep their ageing machinery running, and naturally, the opportunity was embraced.

Of course, a hefty old Camaro still lugging about its factory tub was no match for the latest purpose-built exotics from Germany, even with a big block propelling it along. The better funded teams could actually foot it with the Porsches over a single lap, but couldn't sustain the same race pace, reliability, or fuel economy. That was shown in 1973, when a pair of Camaro victories was largely overshadowed by seven Porsche wins, with the German manufacturer having unleashed its RSR model.

With IMSA stealing the limelight, and the Trans-Am series in disarray, for 1973 the SCCA adopted the exact same regulations as the GT Camel Series, but contested over just six races, and with much less prize money. Of course, it was far less successful.

IMSA continued to grow through 1974, and now boasted factory race teams not only from Porsche, but also BMW, which was both good and bad. While the factory European exotics further raised the profile of IMSA, it meant the domestic machinery, such as the Corvettes and Camaros which had enjoyed success in the series' formative years, were consigned to the role of grid-fillers. Bishop introduced a new class for 1975 called All-American GT, which incorporated tube-frame silhouette variants of domestic models such as the compact Chevrolet Monza and Ford Mustang II, with the intention that they compete head-to-head against the European machinery.

Through it all, the SCCA was having mixed results with its trio of high-profile racing categories launched in 1966 and 1967. The incredible Can-Am Group 7 sports car series ended in 1974, and while Formula 5000 was thriving by the middle of the decade, it was redesigned as a center-seat sports car series for 1976, and renamed as Can-Am.

Somehow, though, the Trans-Am survived. Indeed, by the 1980s it had fully recovered, boasting packed grids and numerous makes and models. While it piggybacked off the IMSA concept for several years, and ventured into a full silhouette formula with tube-frame cars draped in plastic body shells, by the end of the decade it acknowledged the glory days of the 1966-1972 era by introducing a maximum engine size of 5000cc, normally aspirated.

Impressively, the Trans-Am Championship still exists today. Perhaps not surprisingly, among its various classes is one where domestic pony cars including the Ford Mustang, Chevrolet Camaro, and Dodge Challenger compete head-to-head. Although not enjoying manufacturer support to the tune of millions of dollars, or international megastar drivers such as Dan Gurney, Parnelli Jones and Mark Donohue, it is a celebration of the Trans-Am during its brief golden era, only with modern cars and technology. Sadly, like the original golden era, Detroit is again canceling some of its great pony cars and best-known nameplates, as the market naturally ebbs and flows, and buyers' tastes and requirements change.

Perhaps, therefore, the only constant has been the level of interest in the original 1966-1972 SCCA Trans-Am era, and the cars and drivers that competed in it. Although, some of the original drivers are no longer with us, and, indeed, some of the original cars no longer exist, a healthy amount of Trans-Am machinery has not only survived, but been beautifully and lovingly restored to the original liveries and specifications, at great expense, just as they raced in period. They now compete in the Historic Trans-Am group, which hosts anywhere from four to six events each year. While thankfully the cars' enthusiastic owners don't drive them to the extremes of Mark Donohue and Parnelli Jones, they are exercised as per their original intention, not mothballed away from public view. Unlike the original 1966-1972 Trans-Am era, race results are no longer important, and nor is winning. This is a rolling roadshow celebrating one of the greatest periods in American road racing history, and the cars and drivers who made that history.

By the mid-1970s, sedan road racing had a very different look. Former SCCA executive director John Bishop started IMSA, and such was the success of his new venture that the SCCA was forced to abandon its old Trans-Am regulations that dated back to 1966, and adopt the FIA rules used by IMSA. To counter the onslaught of hi-tech European racing machinery, IMSA formulated a new class for domestic vehicles called All American GT. AA-GT allowed for tube-frame chassis design and silhouette body shells. DeKon Engineering, partnered with Chevrolet, built a fleet of these crazy-looking Monzas for the new class. (Courtesy Autosportsltd.com)

GOOD YEAR

International curios

The 1966-1972 era of the Sports Car Club of America Trans-Am series was unique in the way it evolved, very quickly, into a manufacturer war for V8-powered pony cars, starring the big-four US automotive colossals, even if that wasn't the SCCA's original intention.

Although originally intended as an Americanized version of the European Touring Car Championship, pitting various makes and models with varying engine sizes against one another, the influential participation of American manufacturers soon changed the direction and focus of the Trans-Am. This is what made it unique. But the Trans-Am, and the cars competing in it, also had a much broader influence. Interestingly, while the 1966-1972 era is best remembered for its pony car wars, American V8 sedans racing abroad actually predated the series.

Chevrolet Impala

The British Saloon Car Championship began in 1958, and from its inception through to the middle of 1963, every race was won by either a MkI or MkII Jaguar. However, an American interloper threatened to break up the party in 1961, and came within two laps of doing just that.

Dan Gurney, aged 29 and already an established Formula 1 driver, entered the Silverstone International Trophy, Round four of the 1961 BSCC, in the most unlikely of touring car racers: a 409in^3 Chevrolet Impala.

The Impala was the latest 1961 model, with the pretty bubbletop roof. It was ordered with the police/taxi heavy-duty suspension, incorporating beefier springs and shocks, and larger front sway bar. For its new life as a road racer, a Corvette rear sway bar was installed in the back. It also featured 15in-diameter wheels, and Gurney had Bill Thomas (famed for developing top Corvette road racers and later for his Cheetah sports cars) and Bill Fowler go through the motor, which produced 360hp in stock form.

Although lumbered with drum brakes in all four corners, the Impala sported sintered metallic brake pads and Fowler-fabricated brake cooling ducts teamed with flexible hoses. The steel wheels were fitted with wide Goodyear Bluestreak race tires and power steering was also installed.

Although power upgrades were minimal, the sheer cubic mass of the big Chevy's 6.7-liter V8 lump combined with the chassis upgrades simply overwhelmed the Jags in qualifying, and Gurney comfortably claimed pole position for the 12-lap race.

Facing the American entry was a fleet of the latest 3.8-liter MkII Jaguars driven by a squadron of superstar pilots, including Graham Hill, Bruce McLaren, Mike Parkes, and Roy Salvadori.

Come the race and Gurney's big blue Impala left the Jaguars in its wake. Through 10 of the 12 laps, the Chevy wowed the crowds with its thunderous big-block roar, which contrasted with the shrill of the inline Jaguar 6s, and Gurney looked to be cruising to a historic victory. But less than two laps from the end, a wheel broke, and the Impala was out. Hill won from Parkes and McLaren, and the Jaguar juggernaut of the British Saloon Car Championship rolled on.

Opposite top: This was the first American touring car to be raced competitively on the international stage. Dan Gurney commissioned the beautiful Chevy Impala bubbletop, packing a 409in^3 V8, to take on the dominant Jaguars in the British Saloon Car Championship. On debut, the big Chevy would have won, if not for a broken wheel almost within sight of the finish. Dan wasn't invited back. (Courtesy Revs Institute)

Opposite: The Gurney Impala was prevented from competing again in 1961, on the basis of it not having an FIA homologation sheet. But nothing could stop Ford's onslaught two years later when it sent a batch of 427in^3 Galaxies. The first of the Galaxies arrived for Round five of the 1963 British Saloon Car Championship, and from 15 BSCC races contested through 1963 and 1964, Galaxies won 12 of them. (Courtesy Revs Institute)

EXIDE
37

EXPRESS
FERODO
DAILY EXPRESS
LUCAS
SUPER
50

Interestingly, Gurney attempted to race the Impala again in another 1961 BSCC race, now fitted with strengthened NASCAR wheels. But his entry was rejected on the grounds of the Impala having not been homologated as an FIA Group 2 car. Although technically correct, the decision was thought to be politically motivated.

Ford Galaxie

The Jaguar stranglehold on the BSCC was finally broken two years later. In Round five of the 1963 championship, Jack Sears and Sir Gawaine Baillie debuted a pair of monstrous Ford Galaxies which, unlike the Gurney Impala, had been homologated as an FIA Group 2 car. Its homologation sheet featured some interesting upgrades.

The Galaxie was Ford's weapon of choice for the NASCAR Grand National, and with the high-profile NASCAR races being those contested on superspeedways, Ford introduced a mid-year variant of the model: a fastback sports roof to aid greater top speed.

The high-performance Galaxie was propelled by a 427in^3 motor, and while the NASCAR variant was forced to breathe through a single carburetor, the Group 2 model was homologated with twin carburetors. Backing this was a four-speed T-10 transmission, while disc brakes were also listed.

With weight being the Achillies heel of the Galaxie, Ford homologated the Group 2 model with fiberglass doors, front fenders, hood, and deck lid, although ultimately, the glass doors didn't actually appear on the racing variant. Also, the bumpers and bumpers brackets were listed as being pressed from aluminum.

Quite how Ford benefited from having its Galaxies succeed in the British Saloon Car Championship is unclear. After all, the model wasn't sold in Great Britain. But such was the incredible sledgehammer effect of its Total Performance program that Holman Moody was tasked with building the cars and sending them halfway around the world, where a select group of teams would campaign them.

In total, Holman Moody produced four Group 2 lightweight Galaxies – those for the John Willment Group and Sir Gawaine Baillie that appeared in Round five of the BSCC, with Sears winning on debut. A third Galaxie arrived for Round eight of the championship at Brands Hatch. Entered by Alan Brown Racing, it was driven by Jim Clark on debut, and then by Roy Salvadori, Dan Gurney, and Jack Brabham in the races that followed. The fourth Holman Moody Galaxie was sent initially to Ford of France, under which it contested the Tour de France Automobile, before it crossed the Channel to Alan Mann Racing.

The Group 2 Galaxies all rolled on 7x15in steel wheels with double-skinned centers, as per the NASCAR Grand National variants. A limited-slip differential and diff oil cooler were also installed.

An interesting feature (and quite radical for the time) was a robust multipoint roll cage that connected pickup points on the chassis and offered greatly improved rigidity. Although not as complex as a NASCAR cage, it was massively advanced for touring car racing. The Jaguars, for example, featured no roll cage at all. Group 2 regulations required the cars be fitted with full factory interiors, and as such, three bars branched off a central cross-bar connected to the main B-pillar hoop – three aft and one fore. Those going to the rear passed through holes cut into the rear seat. The bar going forward passed across in front of the passenger seat, and required the passenger seat be permanently set in the tilt-forward position, as it couldn't tilt back. With the Galaxies being immediately competitive on debut, the Jaguar teams protested against the roll cages, and ultimately parts of the cage were cut out of them.

Jack Sears started the 1963 season aboard a Ford Cortina GT entered by the John Willment Group. He missed the opening race, as the car wasn't complete. He finished fourth in Round two at Oulton Park, seventh in Round three at Goodwood, and fourth again in Round four at Aintree. At that stage, he really wasn't looking like a championship threat. But he debuted the Willment Group Galaxie in Round five at Silverstone, and won. He also won Round six at Crystal Palace, and Round seven, also held at Silverstone. In Round eight he retired with a punctured tire, and for the final three races, drove the new Willment Lotus Cortina, scoring two thirds and a fourth, and emerged as the 1963 British Saloon Car Champion.

But although Sears had jumped across to a Cortina, Galaxies kept winning the races. Jim Clark won Round eight at Brands Hatch, and Bob Olthoff drove the Willment Galaxie, vacated by Sears, to victory in Round nine. Gurney won Round ten in the Alan Brown Galaxie, and Jack Brabham won the season finale in the same car. Thus, from Round five when the first Galaxies arrived, they won every 1963 race that followed.

The 1964 British Saloon Car Championship was almost as impressive. Galaxies won five of the eight races – Brabham once, Sears four times, but Jim Clark, now driving a Team Lotus-Lotus Cortina, took three victories and won the championship.

For 1965, the British Saloon Car Championship was dominated by the new Ford Mustang, with Alan Mann Racing having built four Group 2 examples which were sold to independent teams. Indeed, Mustangs won six of the eight races, with Clark scoring two victories in the Lotus Cortina. Only one Galaxie appeared in the 1965 BSCC, driven by Alan Hutcheson and which only started Round three at Snetterton, failing to finish.

For 1966, the BSCC switched to FIA Group 5 rules, which offered numerous mechanical freedoms over that of Group 2. The John Willment Group rebuilt its Galaxie, and further lightened it. It entered just four races, driven by Brian Muir. After finishing second to Jack Brabham in an Alan Brown Mustang in Round one, Muir raced the monstrous Galaxie to what would be the model's final BSCC race win in Round two, where he narrowly headed off Brabham, Mike Salmon's Mustang, and Jim Clark's Lotus Cortina. After missing Round three of the championship, Muir and the Galaxie returned for Round four, but a massive shunt in practice ensured the big Ford was not seen again, ending one of the more curious, yet massively successful programs in the history of the British Saloon Car Championship.

Ford Falcon Sprint

As a race car, the Ford Falcon Sprint was almost anonymous in domestic racing competition. And yet, on the international stage, and in particular Great Britain, it had few equals.

Main photo: American muscle to the fore! Pictured at the 1967 British Grand Prix, the BSCC field files through, demonstrating the highly entertaining mixed grids the series boasted. The Falcon Sprint is that of Brian Muir, while Tom Lynch (Camaro), and Bryan Thomson (Mustang) give chase. Having already gone through were Frank Gardner (Alan Mann Racing Falcon Sprint) and Jackie Oliver (Mustang). The Falcon Sprints were all former Monte Carlo Rally cars from 1964, massively rebuilt to FIA Group 5 regulations. (Courtesy Arnold Johnson)

Inset: Certainly the best and fastest of the Group 5 Falcon Sprints that contested the BSCC from 1966-1969. Alan Mann Racing built this example from one of the cars it campaigned on the 1964 Monte Carlo Rally. With a healthy budget of Ford's money, and a workshop packed with exotic GT40 and Cobra parts, this car, in the hands of Australian Frank Gardner, was tough to beat. Gardner won the BSCC in 1967. (Courtesy Chris Bennett)

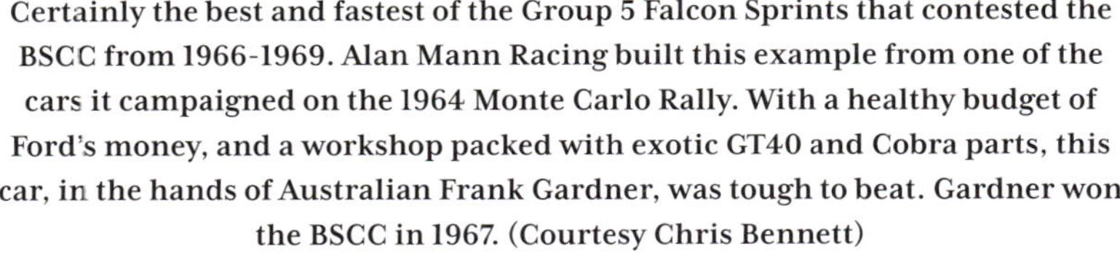

Certainly the best and fastest of the Group 5 Falcon Sprints that contested the BSCC from 1966-1969. Alan Mann Racing built this example from one of the cars it campaigned on the 1964 Monte Carlo Rally. With a healthy budget of Ford's money, and a workshop packed with exotic GT40 and Cobra parts, this car, in the hands of Australian Frank Gardner, was tough to beat. Gardner won the BSCC in 1967. (Courtesy Chris Bennett)

Ford installed the Falcon Sprint into its Total Performance racing program in 1963, with the first-generation model on the Monte Carlo Rally, where it excelled. As per the Group 2 Galaxies, Holman Moody was charged with building the cars. Three were entered in the Monte Carlo, and Swedish racing driver Bosse 'Bo' Ljungfeldt played a starring role. Ljungfeldt won six special stages, but all three Falcons lost so much time during traffic delays resulting from heavily iced roads, that even Ljungfeldt was classified only 43rd at the finish.

However, later in the year, Frenchman Henri Greder drove one of the Falcon Sprints to victory in the Tulip Rally.

When Ford launched its second-generation Falcon for 1964, it went all-out on the homologation sheet. Like the Group 2 Galaxie, the Falcon Sprint, now sporting a larger 289in^3 motor, was homologated with fiberglass front fenders, doors, hood, and deck lid, and Ford listed its minimum weight at a wildly ambitious 980kg (2161 pounds).

Again, Holman Moody produced a fleet of Sprints to be sent across to

In 1968, Alan Mann Racing switched to campaigning Ford Escort Twin-Cams in the BSCC. This was, after all, a Ford of Britain factory team. The Falcon Sprint that Gardner raced to the 1967 BSCC was then acquired by Malcolm Gartlan Racing, and driven by David Hobbs. It kept on winning. (Courtesy Chris Bennett)

Alan Mann Racing, with eight cars entered in the 1964 Monte Carlo. Graham Hill was one of the team drivers, but again it was Bo Ljungfeldt who starred. Ljungfeldt won several special stages, but the points system in 1964 favored small cars, and the rally was ultimately won by Erik Carlsson in a Saab. Ljungfeldt, however, having also won the final speed test (three laps of the Monaco Grand Prix circuit), ultimately finished second outright.

With Ford having launched its new Mustang in April 1964, so it stood down the Falcon from its Total Performance racing program. A team of Mustangs was prepared for the 1964 Liege-Sofia-Liege Rally in August.

With their brief rallying careers at an end, the fleet of Monte Carlo Falcon Sprints returned to Alan Mann Racing, where they were mothballed until re-emerging in 1966 in the British Saloon Car Championship under the new FIA Group 5 regulations.

Group 5 offered numerous freedoms over Group 2, including induction, bodywork, and suspension and brakes. Mustangs dominated the 1965 British Saloon Car Championship and the Falcon Sprint was essentially a Mustang in a different package. But where the Falcon Sprint really offered an advantage was in its homologated 980kg racing weight. Of course, no team ever managed to get a Falcon anywhere near that goal, but certainly, the racing Falcons were lighter than the racing Mustangs.

One by one, Alan Mann Racing sold off its Monte Carlo Sprints, which were rebuilt as Group 5 cars. AMR, however, did keep at least one of the Falcons for itself. This particular car was shared by Peter Jopp and Alain Bertaut on the 1964 Monte Carlo Rally, and was later used as a practice vehicle for Dan Gurney on the Targa Florio.

Although all differing slightly in their delivery, depending largely on the budget each team was packing, the Falcon Sprints all followed a similar theme. The Alan Mann Racing example, however, was surely the best of them, purely because of the stockpile of Ford racing components AMR had at its disposal, and its talented team of engineers. This car underwent significant chassis upgrades, with a new rear cross-member section being fabricated to allow for wider wheels and tires, and rear coil springs in place of leaves. A Watts-link was built to hold the rear end in place under load.

The front suspension uprights were modified and fitted with uniballs in place of rubber bushings, while Girling brakes, sourced from a GT40, were used front and rear, along with Halibrand hubs and three-piece Halibrand GT40 wheels with knock-off pins.

The 289in^3 motor was stroked to 305 cubes, and fitted Gurney-Weslake cylinder heads, a quartet of 48mm two-barrel Weber carburetors mounted on a Cobra intake manifold, and roller rockers. The Group 5 regulations allowed the bumpers to be removed, and they were. The AMR Sprint got down to a reported racing weight of 1060kg (2336-pounds).

Gawaine Baillie and Roy Pierpoint entered Falcon Sprints in the opening round of the 1966 BSCC, and neither made much of an impression in either of the first two races. In Round three, however, the Alan Mann Falcon debuted, driven by John Whitmore, and took an easy victory, with Baillie finishing second. Pierpoint won Rounds 4 and 5, while the brilliant Jim Clark scored the final three victories in a Lotus Cortina.

For 1967, Alan Mann Racing ran the full ten-race schedule, with Frank Gardner driving the team's beautiful red and gold Falcon Sprint. Gardner took seven victories, while Jackie Oliver won the other three in a Mustang. Gardner emerged as the 1967 British Saloon Car Champion.

With AMR being a Ford of Britain factory team, they switched to campaigning a MkII Lotus Cortina in early 1968, until the new Escort Twin-Cam arrived. However, several teams were now racing very quick Falcon Sprints, the most notable of which was Bill Shaw Racing, with driver Brian Muir. He scorched to victory in each of the first five races, while Gardner scored the first win for the new Escort Twin-Cam in Round six. David Hobbs, in the Malcolm Gartlan Racing Falcon Sprint, won Round seven, from Muir. Hobbs and Pierpoint took a win apiece in the two-heat format at the next event, while Muir returned to the victory lane in Round nine, with Pierpoint and Hobbs finishing second and third. Pierpoint won Round ten, while Gardner gave the Escort its second victory in the final.

Gardner ultimately emerged as the champion for the second time.

Pierpoint switched to Bill Shaw Racing in 1969, and continued winning He won four of the first five races (Gardner won the other) before the team debuted a newly built Camaro. After taking a pair of victories, the Bill Shaw Camaro was wrecked in Round ten at Oulton Park where, incidentally, Dennis Leech won the race in another of the Falcon Sprints. Leech also won both heats in Round 11.

The final round of the 1969 British Saloon Car Championship was won by Frank Gardner in the Alan Mann Racing Escort. However, there were five Falcon Sprints in this race, including those for Pierpoint (the team reverting back to the Falcon after the Camaro was destroyed), Leech, David Howes, Terry Sanger, and Martin Birrane.

For 1970, the RAC (Royal Automobile Club) changed the regulations for the BSCC from FIA Group 5 to Group 2, included in which was a five-year cut-off date for all models, with the Falcon Sprint deemed ineligible to continue.

Chevrolet Nova

The Australian Touring Car Championship was contested to FIA Group 2 regulations from 1965 but under the guise of Improved Production, and Norm Beechey became the first driver in Australasia to race a Ford Mustang. He debuted his example in January 1965. A similar example soon followed for Bob Jane.

The ATCC from 1960 through 1968 was contested as a single-race event. In 1965 it was hosted by Sandown Park, in the state of Victoria, on 11 April. Beechey drove through the field after starting 13th to score an impressive victory, overtaking pole-man Jane's Mustang in the process. But by the end of the year, Beechey's Mustang was having a tough time beating the newly built example of Ian Geoghegan, who debuted his Mustang in August. So Beechey opted for a new direction for 1966.

For the that season, Beechey imported and built a Chevrolet Nova (Chevy II), complete with 327in^3 small-block (RPO L79), and the close-ratio four-speed Muncie M21 transmission. The ATCC had no limitations on engine size, and Beechey's plan was to outmuscle the Mustang competition with bigger cubes and more horses.

Norm Beechey, on the hunt at Lakeside Raceway, in Queensland, debuted this beautiful Chevy Nova in 1966 to replace the Mustang he'd used to win the 1965 Australian Touring Car Championship. (Courtesy John Stanley)

For the 1967 season, Beechey repainted the Nova black, with red and yellow stripes for sponsor Shell Oil. He almost won the single-race 1967 ATCC, if not for a punctured tire which fed him into the fence while holding a commanding lead. (Courtesy Mike Feisst)

Beechey ordered a brand-new Chevy II from a Chevrolet dealer in Santa Monica, which arrived in Australia and was rebuilt just in time to make its competition debut at the 1966 ATCC in early April.

The Chevy II wasn't a natural-born road racer, and although homologated by Chevrolet for Group 2 competition, there was clearly little interest from the manufacturer to help it succeed. Indeed, drum brakes, front and rear, were the only option. However, it was a relatively light car, homologated at 2867lb (1300kg), and at least an additional 50hp could be extracted from its 327 Chevy lump over that of the smaller 289in^3 Mustang.

Beechey had at least one motor sent to Traco Engineering before the Chevy II departed the US for Australia. The stout small-block was bored 40-thousand over, and Traco equipped it with much the same internals as the small-block Can-Am motors the company built, as well as a magnesium Moon cross-over intake manifold on which hung a quartet of 58mm Webers two-barrel carburetors. This unit delivered 475hp.

Beechey's Chevy II sported a 12-bolt rear with limited-slip differential. Although consigned to run drum brakes, the team was allowed to drill holes in the backing plates front and rear and fit air ducts to them.

For its early races, the Chevy II rolled on steel NASCAR-style wheels with double-skinned centers, although these were soon replaced with magnesium American Racing Torq Thrust wheels, which not only aided unsprung weight, but also improved brake cooling.

Beechey raced the Chevy II from 1966 through to early 1968, before replacing it briefly with a new Camaro. It won 36 races during that time, however, among them was not the coveted Australian Touring Car Championship.

The 1966 ATCC race was contested on the brutal Mount Panorama track on the outskirts of the small town of Bathurst. At 3.83 miles in length (since extended slightly with the addition of The Chase in 1987), it features a vertical distance between its highest and lowest points of 571ft (174 meters), and the 1.191-mile long Conrod Straight connecting the top of the track to the bottom. It wasn't the ideal place to debut a brand-new car, but Beechey wasn't fazed.

In qualifying, Geoghegan snared pole position from Beechey, who practiced both the Chevy II and his Mustang. However, he opted for the new Chevy come the race.

Beechey's game plan was to blaze away in the opening laps and build a substantial lead over Geoghegan, then hope to maintain that lead as the brakes inevitably gave up. That's precisely what he did. He fired away from the standing start and was leading by 1.3 seconds at the end of the first lap (of 20). And for the first half of the race, Beechey gradually powered off into the distance, to the point of holding a 9.5-second advantage by the end of lap nine.

But then Geoghegan began reeling him in again. He punched out a string of laps over two seconds quicker than Beechey before catching and passing him on lap 15, and drove away to win, while Beechey slowed with a smoking clutch to eventually finish second.

For the 1967 ATCC at Lakeside in Queensland, the roles were reversed. Beechey had a year to further develop the big Chevy while Geoghegan debuted a brand-new 1967 Mustang GTA.

This time the competition was much more fierce, with Bob Jane and Greg Cusack both racing Shelby American Group 2 Mustangs, as were visiting New Zealand drivers Paul Fahey and Norm Barry. Terry Allen, meanwhile, was entered in a new Camaro, powered by a 396in^3 big-block. The short Lakeside circuit would also favor the small-bore machinery, such as Kevin Bartlett's Alfa Romeo GTA.

At qualifying, however, Beechey punched out a confident lap time to claim pole, while Geoghegan sat alongside. From the start, the Chevy II left the competition in its wake, and Beechey knocked out a new lap record on lap three. As the race progressed and his rivals fought among themselves, Beechey was in full control, if nursing a small clutch problem. But on lap 39, of 50, the beautiful Chevy II blew the left rear tire, and after a long slide, smacked the Armco barrier, and was out. Geoghegan, running a distant second, won the race and the championship.

Holden Monaro GTS

Holden was the Australian branch of General Motors (General Motors-Holden). Although it had a long history of assembling British and American vehicles, the first car to carry the Holden name, and be fully Australian-made, arrived in 1948.

Early Australian cars featured ruggedness and practicality over style to cope with the tough local roads and harsh conditions. But in the 1960s, as touring car racing became a prominent form of promotion, and a great way to sell vehicles and build brand loyalty, so performance and styling took hold.

The HK Holden range was launched in 1968, and its various body styles included a four-door sedan, station wagon, utility vehicle (affectionately known as a 'ute' in Australia), panel van, and for the enthusiast, a two-door fastback, called the Monaro.

The Monaro was offered with a broad range of trim, styling, engine and driveline options, the meatiest being the GTS327 model with a 327in^3 small-block Chevrolet V8, backed by a Saginaw four-speed transmission. The GTS

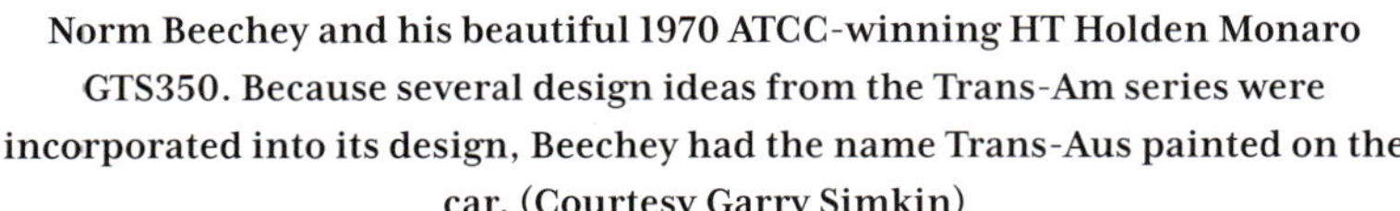

Norm Beechey and his beautiful 1970 ATCC-winning HT Holden Monaro GTS350. Because several design ideas from the Trans-Am series were incorporated into its design, Beechey had the name Trans-Aus painted on the car. (Courtesy Garry Simkin)

Beechey, lifting a wheel as he presses on in the Monaro. This photo was taken at Pukekohe raceway, in New Zealand, where he raced in early 1971 as reigning Australian Touring Car Champion. Note the 10in-wide wheels, which the Australian regulations allowed from 1970. (Courtesy Gerard Richards Collection)

327 was created specifically to win the annual Bathurst 500-mile endurance race, held at Mount Panorama, in which only stock production sedans were eligible to compete.

On debut, the Monaro won Bathurst, after filling the first three positions in qualifying.

However, the Australian Touring Car Championship and Improved Production races were also proving massively popular, and for the newly expanded 1969 ATCC, which featured five races, Norm Beechey built a Monaro GTS327, modified to Improved Production rules.

Having failed to win the ATCC with his charismatic Chevy II, Beechey briefly campaigned a Camaro as a stopgap measure until his Monaro arrived. At a non-championship event in one of its first outings in late 1968, the Beechey's Monaro took victory over Geoghegan's Mustang, which after winning the ATCC on debut in 1967, repeated the feat in 1968. Therefore, much was expected of the new Aussie muscle car in the 1969 ATCC.

Beechey's main rivals in 1969 came from a fleet of American pony cars, including the Mustangs of Geoghegan, Bob Jane, and Allan Moffat. Indeed,

Jane's example was one of the 1968 factory Trans-Am cars run by Shelby Racing Company, and built by Kar-Kraft. Moffat's Mustang was also a Kar-Kraft creation – it was one of the latest 1969 Boss 302 models. Then there were the big-block Camaros of Terry Allen and Bryan Thomson, whose example ran a 600hp 427. At the other end of the scale was the rapid Porsche 911 of Australian Porsche importer Alan Hamilton.

Ultimately, Beechey suffered a frustrating season. He blew the motor in Round one at Calder Park while battling for the lead, while in Round two at Bathurst, he didn't even make the start after smacking the wall during practice, with the damage too severe to repair in time. In Round three at Mallala, Beechey again failed to start the championship race after exploding another motor in a preliminary contest, without enough time to plug in a replacement.

However, his season took an upswing in Round four at Surfers Paradise Raceway, where he won from Hamilton and Jim McKeown's Lotus Cortina, repeating the feat in the final at Symmons Plains. His two victories placed him third in the season standings.

Much better was to come in 1970, however. With a full-tilt horsepower race taking place between Ford Australia and Holden, the latter launched its latest Monaro variant in August 1969: the HT model GTS350. As the name suggests, this new warhorse was propelled by a 350in^3 Chevy V8, and although Holden had Bathurst success in its sights, naturally, this also benefited Beechey's Improved Production plans.

Thus, an all-new car was built for the 1970 ATCC, contested over seven races. Beechey's new Monaro GTS350 was a much improved version of its GTS327 fore-runner. Powering the bright yellow monster was a 350 Chevy bored to 355in^3, with billet crank, forged conrods, and domed Forge-True pistons producing 12.5:1 compression. The heads were locally modified to Traco specifications, and the tough Chevy unit was topped with four 58mm Webers mounted on a cross-ram intake manifold and boasting 550hp. An aluminum Corvette radiator did the cooling.

Beechey had a choice of two different transmissions: a close-ratio Muncie, or a Saginaw with straight-cut gears built by Peter Hollinger. The rear end featured a Chevy 12-bolt limited-slip differential, while the axles were full-floating units.

As per the 1970 SCCA Trans-Am regulations, any type of braking system could be used, and as such, the Monaro was equipped with Corvette four-piston units, as used on the Trans-Am Camaros.

Local CAMS (Confederation for Australian Motor Sports) tweaked the regulations to allow wheel widths to be expanded from 8in in 1969 to 10in, and the Monaro rolled on 15x10in magnesium Minilites. Much focus went into both chassis strength and rigidity, as well as weight loss.

Beechey's 1970 ATCC campaign got off to a rocky start. In the opening race at Calder Park, he started down the grid after a wet qualifying session. But in the race (on a dry track) he simply powered his way through the pack, and quickly dispensed with the Porsche 911s of Brian Foley and Jim McKeown, before blasting past the Mustangs of Jane, Geoghegan, and race leader Moffat. However, he had to stop on the side of the track to pull the fender off the front tire after swiping a lapped car. Once strapped back into the Monaro, Beechey set off again and hunted down leader Moffat again, thundering past him for the second time before being forced to pit and replace the damaged front tire. Although he finished the race (and broke the lap record), he did so outside the points (the ATCC featured the same 9-6-4-3-2-1 system as the Trans-Am).

At Bathurst for Round two, the big, powerful Monaro was a handful, but it was fast! After leading briefly on the first lap, Beechey dropped to third behind Geoghegan and Jane. But he soon left both drivers in his wake with the Monaro enjoying superior straight-line speed over its rivals, and claimed his first ATCC win of 1970.

Sandown Park hosted Round three and Beechey took another win. He grabbed pole position, led the race from start to finish, and blitzed the lap record in the process. As such, he was leading the championship after two rounds, with 18 points.

Foley took pole position from Beechey in Round four at Mallala, but Moffat swept to the front amid rain early in the race, holding a commanding lead until the rain stopped and the track dried. Beechey worked his way back to second, until a slipping clutch slowed his progress, allowing Geoghegan and Foley past. When Moffat's clutch failed, and Foley pitted with handling issues, Beechey was promoted up to second behind winner Geoghegan.

McKeown won Round five at Warwick Farm, which featured a multicar wreck at the first turn, including the Mustangs of Geoghegan and Moffat, as well as the Porsches of Foley and Bill Brown. This promoted Beechey to second, although he couldn't match McKeown's pace. However, he lost six valuable points when a rear wheel departed.

The next race at Lakeside produced another big wreck, this time involving Mustang racer Chris Brauer, just after the start. Escaping the chaos, Geoghegan grabbed the lead from Beechey, while McKeown, Moffat, Brown and Jane gave chase. And while others around him faltered, Beechey only surged forward, taking the lead from Geoghegan, and holding it to the end. And with another nine points in his pocket, and only one round remaining, Beechey's championship lead couldn't be beaten.

One of two Ford 'Super Falcons', crafted by Ford Australia, with the intention of winning the Australian Touring Car Championship. The Aussie Falcon was effectively a third-generation American Falcon, but built in Australia in right-hand drive, and including several design and styling features for the Australian market. This particular car was built for Canadian-born Allan Moffat, who moved to Australia on a full-time basis in 1969, taking a new Kar-Kraft Boss 302 Mustang with him. Moffat's Super Falcon was painted in the same colors as his Mustang, and was intended to be the Mustang's replacement, but that never happened. (Courtesy Perry Drury)

The second of the Super Falcons was built for Ian 'Pete' Geoghegan, and painted in the colors of the Mustang he was already campaigning. Unlike Moffat, Geoghegan persisted with his Super Falcon beyond 1971, and after a huge development program to make the chassis more rigid, Geoghegan raced the 615hp monster to a single ATCC victory, at Bathurst in 1972. (Courtesy Perry Drury)

That was a good thing, because his engine blew in practice for the final race at Symmons Plains and he couldn't start the race. It didn't matter; Beechey won his second ATCC, while Holden scored its first. It was the first of many.

Beechey continued racing the Monaro in 1971 and 1972, but the competition had stepped up its game, with just a single victory in Round two of the 1971 championship being the only highlight.

Ford Falcon GT-HO

The importance of the Australian Touring Car Championship during the late 1960s, and its ability to sway race fans toward certain winning manufacturers' products, prompted Ford Australia to launch an ambitious program to build a pair of factory-supported Falcon GT-HOs for Allan Moffat and Ian Geoghegan. With Beechey flying the Holden flag in the ATCC, so Ford understood the importance of its locally produced Falcon – not the imported Mustang – being its crown jewel in the ATCC.

Ford Australia began producing the Falcon in 1960. It was, very much, a right-hand-drive version of the American Falcon, but including a handful of improvements for the sake of robustness to deal with Australian roads.

The first-generation Australian Falcon continued until 1966, and increasingly featured local design influence that distinguished it from its American counterpart. Unlike the US version, there was no V8 offered.

The second-generation model was based on the third-generation American Falcon. And finally, as performance was becoming an increasingly important marketing tool, so a V8 was finally introduced.

Interestingly, while Ford North America restored the Falcon to its original role as a budget-focused all-rounder, and pushed the Mustang as its performance model, Ford Australia went the opposite route. Although appearing almost identical, aside from some minor styling changes, the second-generation Australian and third-generation Falcons looked very similar. But the Aussie model now made a notable shift with the launch of the first Falcon GT, which Ford Australia created specifically to win the 1967 Bathurst 500-mile endurance race.

Also of interest was the fact the Falcon GT was only available as a four-door model. Ford Australia chose not to produce a two-door Falcon.

Ford Australia branded its various Falcon models using a pair of letters (Holden did likewise), starting with the original 1960 variant, which was called the XK. There followed the XL, XM, and XP to round out the first-generation, while the second-generation began as the XR. The XR Falcon GT was launched in May 1967, powered by the 289in^3 Ford Windsor V8. Among its various upgrades were improved brakes and suspension, four-speed Ford Toploader transmission, while the 289 featured a performance camshaft raised compression (9.8:1), was topped with a four-barrel carburetor, and breathed through a free-flowing exhaust.

And it won. Falcon GTs finished first and second in the 1967 Bathurst 500.

In May 1968, Ford Australia released the XT model Falcon GT, which boasted several improvements over its predecessor, including a larger 302, which packed more power. However, it didn't pack as much power as Holden's new Monaro GTS327, which not only qualified in the first three positions at Bathurst in 1968, but also filled the podium positions at the race. Indeed, the first Falcon home was seventh.

Ford unveiled the XW model Falcon GT-HO (Handling Option) in August 1969, which was equipped with a 351in^3 Windsor V8 producing 300hp. As well as a focused performance suspension and brake package, front spoiler, and hood scoop that ducted cool air to the brake master cylinder, the GT-HO (and regular Falcon GT) featured a lurid stripe package that included a 'Super Roo' Kangaroo cartoon character on the front fenders.

Against the new Monaro GTS350, the GT-HO looked like the package to beat at Bathurst in 1969. The example shared by Geoghegan brothers Ian and Leo took pole position, and there were six GT-HOs that qualified in the top ten. However, a multi-car wreck on the opening lap eliminated several GT-HOs, and throughout the race, the surviving examples destroyed their tires. A quirk of the Bathurst regulations, under the guise Series Production, was that each class in the race was decreed by a retail price range. Because Ford wanted to pit the Falcon against the Monaro, it fitted the GT-HO with 14in 12-slot steel wheels, as found on the 1969 Mustang Mach-1. And the power of the big Windsor V8 simply ate tires.

In the end, Holden won the 1969 Bathurst epic.

For 1970, Ford introduced the XW Falcon GT-HO Phase II, which differed only slightly from the original version, aside from the new 351 Cleveland replacing the outgoing Windsor.

With seven GT-HO Phase IIs qualifying in the top ten, including the first three positions, Ford returned to glory by winning the 1970 Bathurst 500, taking first and second.

In September 1971, the new GT-HO Phase III arrived, based on the facelifted XY Falcon model, and was again an overall improvement over the Phase II. Its most notable feature was a shaker scoop mounted over and feeding cool air to the carburetor through a hole cut in the hood. Like many of the Australian Falcon performance upgrades, this was an item borrowed from the Mustang.

At Bathurst in 1971, Falcon GT-HO Phase IIIs filled the first seven positions on the grid, and after 500 epic racing miles, the first three places in the race.

It was this kind of success, and most importantly, upstaging rival Holden, that Ford wanted to carry across to the Australian Touring Car Championship in 1970 under the Improved Production rules.

In early 1970, work began on two XW Falcons at Ford Special Vehicles. These cars were quickly dubbed 'Super Falcons'. Al Turner was the Ford Australia racing boss at the time, and he sourced a set of blueprints from Kar-Kraft for the factory Trans-Am Mustangs, with the intention that they be adapted to the Falcon platform. In the end, this process proved both costly and ineffective, and FSP simply adapted the Falcons using its own racing knowledge, just as Norm Beechey had done with the Holden Monaro.

Ford Australia under Al Turner was a no-compromise heavyweight when it came to racing, and packed a healthy budget. Like the Trans-Am cars, the Super Falcons featured body components which were acid-dipped to reduce weight, while the motors were moved back in the chassis, with the carefully reprofiled firewalls offering a small amount of additional space. Improved Production rules required cars be fitted with full interiors, so the Super Falcons had anything that wasn't visible to tech inspectors drilled to reduce weight, while many of the components visible were recast from lighter materials. The door hinges, for example, were made from magnesium. Front and rear bumpers were stamped from thin-gauge metal. Nothing was overlooked in an effort to save weight. Even the wheel nuts were made from titanium.

The Super Falcons featured several tricks to aid in maintenance and/or repair, including a front cross-member that could be quickly removed so the sump could be dropped out while the engine remained in place. The radiator support panels were also quick-release items so the motor could be quickly removed out the front.

Ultimately, the Super Falcons weighed 2900lb (1315kg) compared with a stock Ford Falcon GT at 3268lb.

Perhaps the most impressive feature were the motors. These were based on the Cleveland V8, and fitted with heads sourced from Falconer & Dunn, then further modified and fitted with aluminum roller rockers and titanium valves.

Improved Production regulations allowed for fuel-injection, and the Super Falcon motors sported beautiful Lucas mechanical systems that were adapted and fitted with eight curved intake trumpets, designed to fit beneath the stock hood.

The motors packed 12.5:1 pistons and special conrods machined from Repco Formula 1 castings. The Super Falcon motors also used dry-sump systems with a four-stage Weaver scavenger pump.

All told, the Super Falcons hit the track with 570hp in late 1970, but this was improved upon over the next two years.

Behind the modified Ford Toploader four-speed transmission, the rear axle arrangement included a Detroit Locker limited-slip, full-floating axles, and Watts-link, while adjustable Koni shocks were used front and rear. While retaining leaf springs in the rear, as per the street Falcon, those on the Super Falcons were made from aluminum, and were much narrower than stock, to allow for the fat wheels and tires the cars would wear. Under the new-for-1970 rules, the Super Falcons rolled on 15x10in magnesium Minilite wheels.

Front brakes were Kelsey-Hayes, similar to those used on the Trans-Am Mustangs. Weight saving continued inside the cars, with front bucket seats patterned from those of the Ford GT40, as well as a bolt-in roll cage. The two Super Falcons were painted red for Moffat, and white for Geoghegan, the same as their existing Mustangs.

Following various delays in the program, the first of the Super Falcons – Moffat's red car – made its first competition appearance in the final round of the 1970 ATCC at Calder Park. Despite only running four laps before the motor blew, Moffat produced a qualifying time fast enough to put him on pole.

Development continued through the Australian off-season, but come the first race of the 1971 ATCC, neither car appeared, as ongoing delays and troubleshooting continued. Moffat arrived at Calder Park for Round two with his Super Falcon and Kar-Kraft Mustang. The Falcon was now sporting a new XW model grille and stripe package. After running qualifying laps in both cars, he opted to race his Mustang, which had been circulating two seconds faster.

For Round three at Sandown Park, both Super Falcons appeared for the first time. After trialing their Falcons and Mustangs, the pair chose to race their American Fords. Moffat again took both cars to Surfers Paradise for Round four (Geoghegan only took his Mustang), and again the Mustang was faster. However, local driver John French was called upon to qualify and race the Super Falcon. Moffat proved his decision was correct, and went on to win, while French ultimately finished fourth, behind Bob Jane's newly built 1969 Camaro ZL1, and Geoghegan.

Neither Super Falcon appeared at Mallala for Round five, but both made the trip to Queensland for Round six at Lakeside Raceway. Again, both drivers chose to race their Mustangs, and again, French was called upon to drive a Super Falcon (this time it was Geoghegan's car). He finished fifth.

Ian's brother Leo tested the white Super Falcon for the final round at Oran Park but chose not to race it. Moffat didn't even bother taking his. And with that, the season concluded with neither of the hugely expensive Super Falcons really making any impression on the American pony car opposition, or even Norm Beechey's year-old Monaro.

Ford Australia effectively abandoned the Super Falcon program at the conclusion of 1971, as the all-new third-generation Falcon was due to be launched later that year, and pumping money into a racing program for a model about to be superseded made little sense. Therefore, both Super Falcons were gifted to Moffat and Geoghegan, to do with as they pleased.

For 1972, Moffat completely gave up on his car and focused efforts on his Mustang. All valuable and useful parts were scavenged, some of which found their way into his Mustang, and the remains were scrapped.

Geoghegan, however, didn't enjoy the luxury of a competitive Kar-Kraft Mustang to fall back on. He was still campaigning the notchback GTA model he debuted in 1967, and it had reached the end of its shelf life. His only real option was to somehow make his Super Falcon work. So he began an intensive development program to not only coax even more power from the fuel-injected mill, but also to improve its handling. One of the biggest problems with the Super Falcons was that, in an effort to shed as much weight as possible, chassis rigidity had been massively compromised.

A much more robust and complex roll cage was constructed and welded in place. The body was also seam-welded, while a new rear subframe was installed to provide more strength. Meanwhile, horsepower was increased to over 600.

The 1972 ATCC was contested over eight rounds, starting in Tasmania, at Symmons Plains. Geoghegan qualified fifth in a wet practice, but at the start, powered his way up to second behind Moffat. However, he pitted at the end of the first tour with something amiss in the rear suspension. After a quick check, he bolted back out and, within eight laps, had recovered to fourth, but ultimately retired with an overheating engine.

In Round two at Calder Park, Geoghegan qualified third but again pitted early, this time to check an oil leak. Once going again, he powered his way back through the field to finish third. This was the best result yet for a Super Falcon. But better was to come.

Round three was at Bathurst, and Geoghegan qualified second to Moffat. From the flag, Bob Jane jumped to the front from the second row in his Camaro, but was soon relegated, first by Moffat, then Geoghegan. Very quickly, the red Mustang and white Falcon shot away to fight their own battle for the lead, and on lap three, up the steep Mountain Straight, Geoghegan used the extra grunt of the Super Falcon's 600hp to romp past Moffat.

For lap after lap, the pair traded places, with Geoghegan muscling his way past on the straights, and Moffat regaining the position under braking. From early in the race, Moffat was struggling to see due to oil from Geoghegan's catch tank smearing across his windshield, which Moffat made worse by instinctively putting his wipers on. To help see better, he loosened his harness, then removed it altogether so he could peer out the side window.

As the laps wound down the battle intensified, and both drivers were lapping significantly faster than their qualifying times. Indeed, Geoghegan was hitting 185mph down the long Conrod Straight.

On the final lap the pair braked hard into the final turn, and Geoghegan went in deeper than he had done before, forcing Moffat to downshift into first gear in an effort to make a faster exit and beat the Falcon to the line. This, however, flooded the carburetors, and Geoghegan got there first, by six tenths of a second. It was the first ATCC win for the Super Falcon. Indeed, it would prove to be the car's only ATCC win.

In Round four at Sandown Park, Geoghegan qualified second and was running third in the race before retiring with mechanical troubles. Fuel pressure issues thwarted his charge in Round five at Adelaide International Raceway, but he went the full distance, finishing third. Geoghegan was a non-starter for Round six at Warwick Farm after the Super Falcon bent a valve in practice and a replacement couldn't be sought in time. The team straightened the bent valve for the race, but the car was already smoking on its way to the start, and officials forced Geoghegan to withdraw.

Geoghegan didn't attend Round seven at Surfers Paradise, but returned for the final at Oran Park. Now sporting yellow paint, and a rebuilt motor producing 615hp, he put the Super Falcon on pole. From the start he romped away and established a commanding lead, only for the motor to start cutting out through left-hand corners. Eventually, Moffat caught him and slipped past with just three laps remaining.

With that, the final curtain lowered on Ford Australia's ambitious Improved Production Falcon program. Geoghegan ultimately finished fourth in the 1972 ATCC drivers' standings, and after two years and a pile of money funneled into the project, a single ATCC race win fell well short of Ford's expectations. Although Geoghegan developed his car into a genuine contender throughout 1972, new regulations deemed it ineligible to compete in 1973.

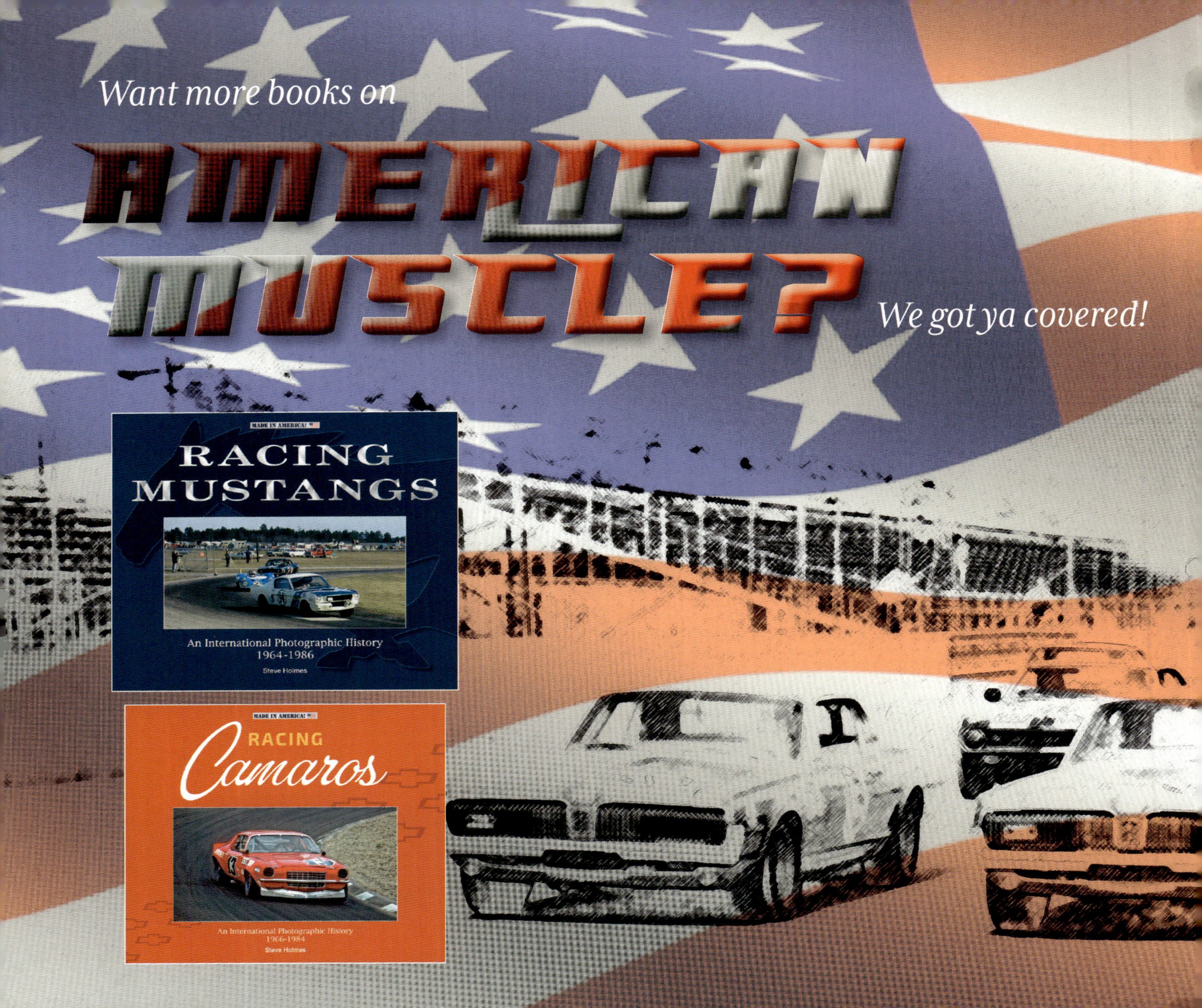

Want more books on
AMERICAN
MUSCLE?
We got ya covered!
MADE IN AMERICA!
RACING
MUSTANGS
An International Photographic History
1964-1986
Steve Holmes
MADE IN AMERICA!
RACING
Camaros
An International Photographic History
1966-1984
Steve Holmes

MOPAR MUSCLE
ARRACUDA, DART & VALIANT
60 TO 1980
RC CRANSWICK
EWORD BY DON GARLITS

FORD
MUSTANG II
& PINTO
1970 to 1980

MARC CRANSWICK
FOREWORD BY JOHN H DAVIS

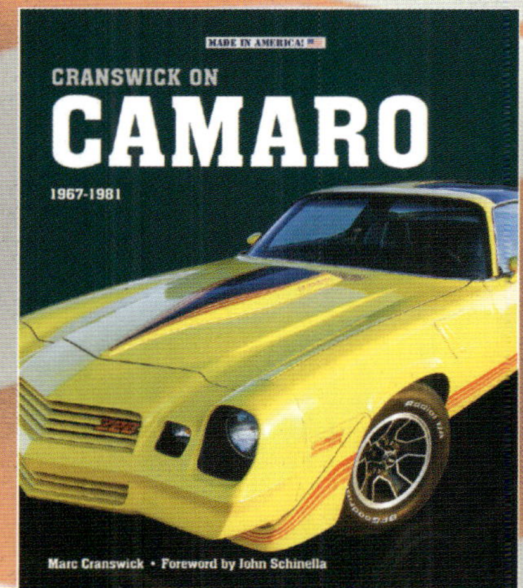
MADE IN AMERICA!
CRANSWICK ON
CAMARO
1967-1981
Marc Cranswick • Foreword by John Schinella

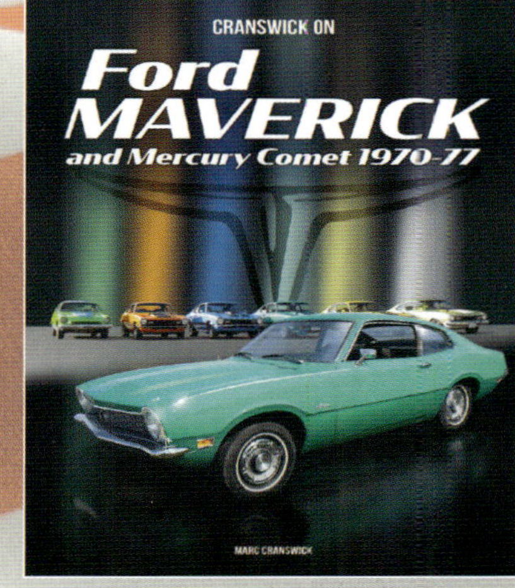
CRANSWICK ON
Ford
MAVERICK
and Mercury Comet 1970-77
MARC CRANSWICK

The Legend of
American
Motors
The full history of America's most innovative automaker
Marc Cranswick

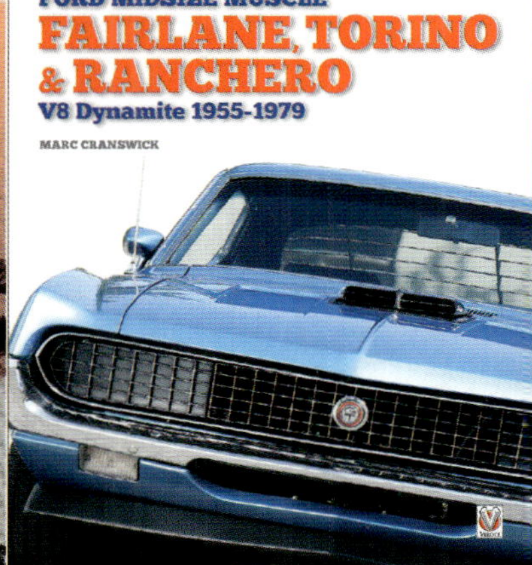
FORD MIDSIZE MUSCLE
FAIRLANE, TORINO
& RANCHERO
V8 Dynamite 1955-1979
MARC CRANSWICK

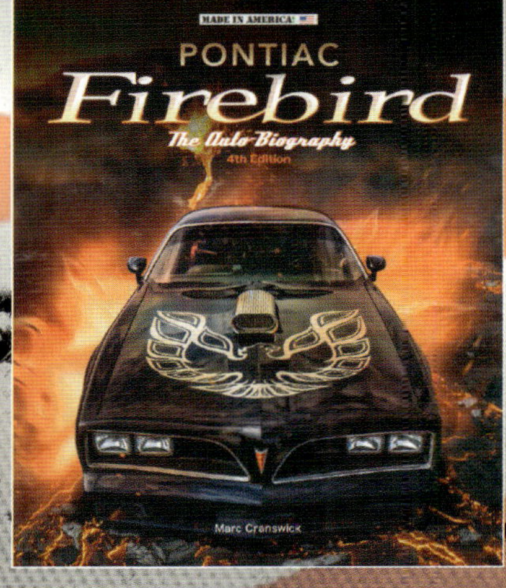
MADE IN AMERICA!
PONTIAC
Firebird
The Auto-Biography
4th Edition
Marc Cranswick

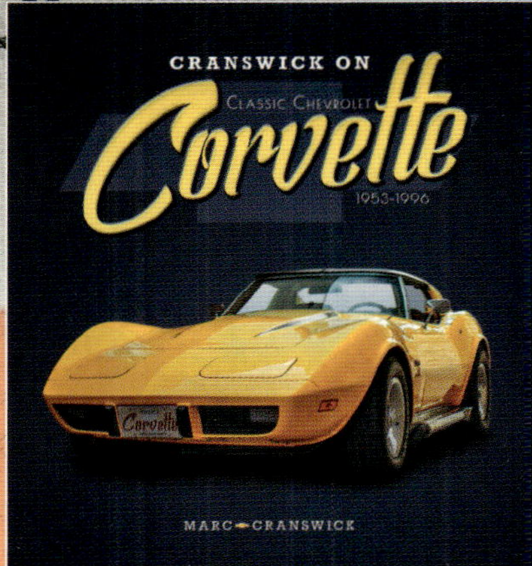
CRANSWICK ON
CLASSIC CHEVROLET
Corvette
1953-1996
MARC CRANSWICK

Index